TRUE NORTH, STRONG AND FREE

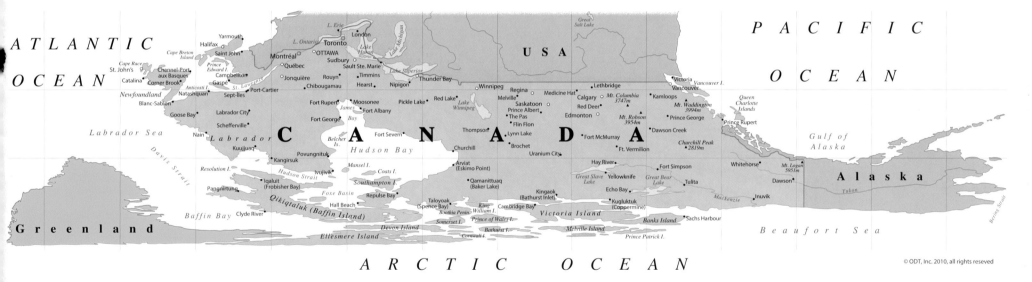

ATLANTIC OCEAN

PACIFIC OCEAN

Labrador Sea

Davis Strait

Greenland

Baffin Bay

C A N A D A

Hudson Bay

ARCTIC OCEAN

Gulf of Alaska

A l a s k a

Beaufort Sea

Yarmouth, Halifax, Cape Breton Island, Saint John, Cape Race, St. John's, Channel-Port aux Basques, Prince Edward I., Campbellton, Catalina, Corner Brook, Anticosti I., Gaspé, Montréal, OTTAWA, Sudbury, Québec, Jonquière, Rouyn, Sault Ste. Marie, Chibougamau, Hearst, Timmins, Nipigon, Thunder Bay, Newfoundland, Natashquan, St. Lawrence, Port-Cartier, Sept-Îles, Blanc-Sablon, Goose Bay, Labrador City, Fort Rupert, Moosonee, Pickle Lake, Red Lake, Lake Winnipeg, Winnipeg, Regina, Medicine Hat, Lethbridge, Victoria, Vancouver I., Vancouver, Melville, Saskatoon, Calgary, Mt. Columbia 3747m, Kamloops, Mt. Waddington 3994m, Queen Charlotte Islands, Schefferville, Fort George, James Bay, Fort Albany, Red Deer, Prince Albert, The Pas, Edmonton, Mt. Robson 3954m, Prince George, Nain, Labrador, Belcher Is., Fort Severn, Thompson, Flin Flon, Lynn Lake, Fort McMurray, Dawson Creek, Prince Rupert, Kuujjuaq, Churchill, Brochet, Churchill Peak 2819m, Kangirsuk, Povungnituk, Uranium City, Ft. Vermilion, Resolution I., Ivujivik, Mansel I., Arviat (Eskimo Point), Hay River, Fort Simpson, Whitehorse, Mt. Logan 5951m, Pangnirtung, Iqaluit (Frobisher Bay), Hudson Strait, Coats I., Southampton I., Qamanittuaq (Baker Lake), Great Slave Lake, Yellowknife, Great Bear Lake, Echo Bay, Tulita, Dawson, Hall Beach, Repulse Bay, Kingaok (Bathurst Inlet), Kugluktuk (Coppermine), Mackenzie, Inuvik, Qikiqtaluk (Baffin Island), Clyde River, Taloyoak (Spence Bay), King William I., Cambridge Bay, Victoria Island, Banks Island, Sachs Harbour, Foxe Basin, Boothia Penin., Somerset I., Prince of Wales I., Bathurst I., Melville Island, Prince Patrick I., Baffin Bay, Devon Island, Cornwall I., Ellesmere Island, Yukon, Bering Strait

USA

L. Erie, L. Ontario, Lake Huron, Lake Michigan, Lake Superior, Great Salt Lake, Toronto, London

TRUE NORTH, STRONG AND FREE
New Ways of Looking at Canada on the 150th Birthday of the Country

Brian Arthur Brown

With Foreword Material by the National Chief of the Assembly of First Nations
Perry Bellegarde

An Introduction and Maps Curated by
Ward Kaiser

And Contributions by National Political and Community Leaders

Preface One by Elizabeth May, Leader of the Green Party of Canada

Preface Two by Ward Kaiser, Curator of Maps for this volume

Preface Three by The Hon. Rob Nicholson, Conservative MP for Niagara

Preface Four by The Hon. Larry Bagnell, Liberal MP for Yukon

Preface Five by The Rt. Rev. David W. Parsons, Bishop of the Arctic

Printed in Canada at the presses of Marquis Imprimeur, Montmagny, Quebec
Published by 3T Publishing, 5195 Rosedale Drive, Niagara Falls, ON L2E 1R7

Canadian Cataloguing-in-Publication data:
Brown, Brian Arthur 1942 –
True North, Strong and Free / Brian Arthur Brown
Complete cataloguing data available from Library and Archives Canada

Library of Congress Cataloguing-in-Publication data:
Brown, Brian Arthur 1942 –
True North, Strong and Free / Brian Arthur Brown
    1. Canada,   2. Sesquicentennial, 3. First Nations,   4. Arctic,   5. Domed Cities   6. Turks and Caicos

ISBN 978-0-9936942-3-3

Front Cover: *Our Home and Native Land* With Swiss, German, French Canadian, and Ukrainian ancestry, the artist, Jen Adomeit, is a Canadian with no Indigenous ancestry. Fascinated by the striking artistic style of the Northwest Coast First Nations in the part of British Columbia where she grew up, she studied First Nations art while attending UNBC and painted this "interpretative representation" there in 2006. The official animal of each province is embodied in a stylized map which illustrates both the First Nations affinity with the land and its creatures and the European practice of dividing the land into "productive" political units of management. Both appear necessary for the environment and the human economy to coexist in harmony – one of the "new ways of looking at Canada" in this book which promotes First Nations self-government and respect for creation on the part of all Canadians. To order this artwork, see information under Illustrations on page 131.

Back Cover: These images by Salvador Ayala suggest a mosque in the Western Arctic, an inukshuk erected in Niagara by the author in 2006, and the "Igloo Cathedral" in the Eastern Arctic, all evocative of new Canadian perspectives in their respective locations.

Table of Contents

A Dedication to Peace in the Dwelling Places

Kanata

As evidenced by the sixteenth century journal of Jacques Cartier in his voyage to Stadacona, present-day Québec City, Canada's name is derived from the Iroquoian word, "kanata," which holds the same meaning in Mohawk and Oneida, and can be translated as "Dwelling Places." The native imprint on Canada is as indelible as that name and other names like those from our largest city to the smallest villages and the national capital. But Canada will never fulfill its grand potential until full participation of the native population becomes the reality envisioned by treaties long-forgotten by governments, land claims currently before the courts, and through implementation of the Report on Truth and Reconciliation by the citizens of Canada.

A Mari Usque Ad Mari

"Et dominabitur a mari usque ad mari, et a flumine usque ad terminos terrae," in the Latin of the Vulgate Bible, is the basis of the national motto of Canada (English: *From Sea to Sea*; French: *D'un océan à l'autre*). Psalm 72:8 is translated in the King James Version of the Bible as "And he shall have dominion from sea to sea, and from the river unto the ends of the earth," referring to our dominion under God from the Atlantic to the Pacific, and from the St. Lawrence and Great Lakes to the North Pole. This stewardship of the land, the water, the air and all the creatures of our country is a responsibility of all Canadians as led by Canada's First Nations.

The Constitution of Canada

"Canada is founded upon principles that recognize the supremacy of God and the rule of law." So says The Canadian Charter of Rights and Freedoms in the Introduction to the Constitution of Canada. To perhaps over simplify a comparison of ethos between two competing national ideologies in North America, while God is nowhere mentioned in the American constitution, an acknowledgement of the Divine order is fundamental to the Canadian Constitution.

As a result, Americans appears to be always scrambling to assert their religiosity, whereas in Canada the practice of religion is less overt, but God is presumed to be omnipresent. At the same time, while Canadian law respects the rights of each religion (important in an era when First Nations and New Canadians offer increasing levels of religious devotion, as will be seen in this book), the law itself also defends the rights of persons who practice or profess no religion.

The Order of Canada

During the 1967 centennial of confederation, Canada established a three-tiered order to recognize distinguished citizens who make major contributions to the country in various fields of endeavor, as well as non-Canadians who have made the world better by their activities. Membership is symbolized by a medal presented by the Governor General in the name of the monarch to those who epitomize the motto of the order, *desiderantes meliorem patriam*, a biblical phrase from Hebrews 11:16, meaning "they desire a better country." Originally referring to Abraham, Sarah and others in search of "The Promised Land" it could also refer to the original aboriginal nomads who came here from Siberia and the pioneer settlers from France, Britain and loyalists from the USA, followed by others from every corner of the globe, desiring a better country.

The Peace Tower

Few human constructs embody the Canadian vision better than the buildings of parliament with the Peace Tower and its inscription, *Where There is no Vision, the People Perish*, taken directly from Proverbs 29: 18 in the King James Version of the Bible. A myriad of such quotations are chiseled into the foundation stones of our democracy, about half from the Jewish section of the Bible, and half from the Christian. A certain perverse "politically correct" impulse in our increasingly mixed society might seek to obliterate such foundational inscriptions, but given the spirituality of most current immigrants, a more "spiritually correct" alteration in 2017 would be to commission appropriate inscriptions from five more of the seven recognized world religions, as well as various traditional religions. Added in renovations to parliamentary buildings, and enhanced by native spiritual artwork, such greetings of peace might even include some blank stones to symbolize the outlook of any who claim no spiritual heritage.

Greetings of Peace

Assalamu alaikum is a common greeting among Muslims, meaning "Peace be with you." Hindus chant the peace mantra, *Om: Shanti, Shanti, Shanti* and Buddhists reply, *Embrace the Tranquility of Peace*. Taoists urge us to *Watch over the Workings of all Creation*, and Confucius says *When the personal life is cultivated the family life is regulated; when the family life is regulated then the national life is orderly; and when the national life is orderly there is peace in this world*. We can no doubt improve this list before we get out our chisels, but New Canadians soon learn that rather than fight about such issues, in Canada we prefer to "appoint a Royal Commission," a committee to discuss it to exhaustion, at which point something "spiritually correct" materializes. This is our traditional alternative to war. It is cheaper and works well in Canada; we commend it to the rest of the world.

Maintiens le Droit

Adoption of the Norman French motto (translated as "defending the right"), gave the RCMP a bilingual character from the very beginning. La devise officielle de la Gendarmerie "Maintiens le Droit" est un diction qui est autour depuis le 14ème siècle, quand il a été utilise par plusieurs familles en Grande-Bretagne."

We build on Native origins, respect our official languages and encourage others, expand our multicultural heritages and engage in international relations, all within secure borders, which brings us to the topic at hand, celebrating the past and mapping the future in a present that while not smug, is certainly joyful.

O Canada
God keep our land, glorious and free.

What Does Canada Really Look Like?

This souvenir book celebrates Canada's dynamic history, the exciting opportunities of Canada's present, and looks to Canada's promising future.

The true map of Canada will be reproduced in 26 views of this country from every angle to show a constantly changing Canada in the 19th, 20th and 21st centuries.

This is not the image of the country most adult Canadians grew up with. It is a computer generated "area-accurate" map, like those used now in schools, showing the correct size and shape of Canada.

On the familiar but wrong older version of the map (huge copies hanging in the constituency offices of most members of Parliament and elsewhere) the globe got splayed out over the north in a stretched distortion required to fill a flat rectangular shaped map.

Our more manageable Canada (a shape also seen on any globe) points to a fulfilling future for our country in more sustainable development. This is a dramatic new vision.

Let's start by looking at Canada on page one. It represents Canada as seen from the North Pole, which makes more sense to us than looking at our country from the equator. It shows the true shape and the actual square kilometres of northern areas, rather than the distortions of the north seen on most traditional maps. Many adult Canadians do not actually know the size and the shape of our country.

Indeed, most Canadians think of Canada on a wall map as stretching from the forty-ninth parallel north to almost infinity, and almost as wide as tall.

In fact, Canada is a thousand kilometres wider east-to-west than tall south-to-north. This is a short plump country, not much like the far north colossus we thought we knew.

Modern classrooms give more accurate presentations to young Canadians and this book is intended to remedy the situation for their parents and grandparents in the sesquicentennial year, celebrating the 150th anniversary of confederation. In the same spirit we take a fresh look at First Nations, the changing face of religion, business enterprise, our military record, sporting achievements, Canadian inventions, our place in the world and other aspects of life in Canada in this sesquicentennial year.

Commentators helping us with this fresh perspective on Canada include three political leaders and three from broader Canadian culture. Elizabeth May, Leader of the Green Party of Canada is from East and West, Cape Breton and Vancouver Island. Larry Bagnell, MP for Yukon, is a member of the Liberal Party of Canada. Rob Nicholson, MP for Niagara Falls, is a member of the Conservative Party of Canada. Ward Kaiser, our academic advisor and map curator, happens to also represent an NDP perspective. Perry Bellegarde is the National Chief of the Assembly of First Nations. David Parsons is the Anglican Bishop of the Arctic. Together with the author they represent all parts of Canada, North, South, East, West and Central.

CANADA: A NORTH POLE PERSPECTIVE

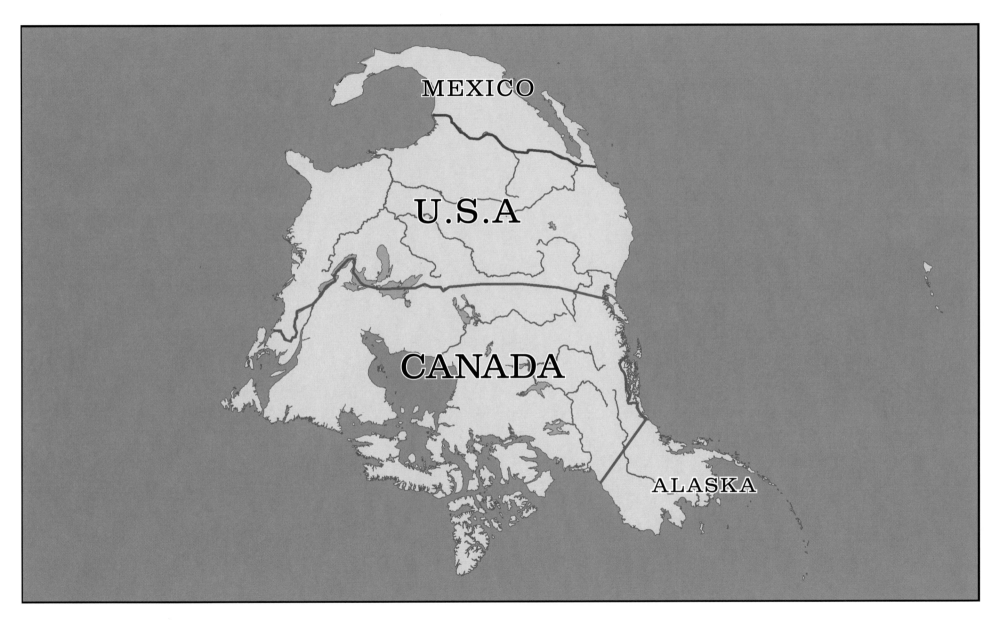

Map A: Canada Seen from the North Pole: Wide, not Tall, and with a Land Mass Actually Smaller than the USA

What is So Special About Canadians?

Born of an abused Aboriginal mother and an orphaned French father, in a political marriage arranged by the British crown, the family of Canada expanded with adopted siblings running away from home in Ireland's punishing "ethnic cleansing" by corn laws and potato famine, Scotland's switch from people to sheep in the "highland clearances," and New England refugees from the American revolution, who called themselves "United Empire Loyalists." Pennsylvania Deutsch settlers came to farm when good land ran short in the USA, and Chinese laborers came for risky work building a railroad and stayed to run businesses like restaurants and laundries at first. More sons and daughters were adopted into the family from Ukraine where they were oppressed under Austrian and Russian rule, followed by "Displaced Persons" from Central and Eastern Europe on the losing side of pointless wars, including Poles, Germans, Dutch and Jews. These political refugees were succeeded by economic refugees from Italy, Greece and Portugal, followed by Hungarians, again fleeing Russian oppression.

The Japanese struggled to gain acceptance here but persevered in professions and fishing, as did grudgingly admitted Sikhs, who prospered in lumbering and agriculture.

They opened the doors for Hindus and Muslims of India and Pakistan, as well as Africans, white and black, and Indians from East Africa fleeing the dictator Idi Amin. With the fall of the Soviet Union, Russians came mainly from former Soviet lands where they had become *persona non gratia* after years of privilege. Iraqi and Afghan refugees next joined Mexicans and other Hispanics escaping conflicts in the Americas. As the sesquicentennial celebrations begin, Canada is blessing itself by integrating Syrians fleeing battle. These hard working young families join previous Middle Easterners from places like Egypt, Turkey and Lebanon, Muslims and others now in political leadership in Canada from places like Charlottetown "down east" to Calgary "out west," building our country from Cape Breton to Yukon.

This accounts for the much vaunted multiculturalism our politicians are fond of boasting about, but does not explain how we get along together so well in such diversity. The key to that lies in another trait of this country. If the national ethos of Australia was that of convicts building a new country, and if the Statue of Liberty invites the world to "send us your poor" who prospered in the USA, what do those who came to Canada have in common? In truth, most of us came here after being on the losing side of a battle with tyrants somewhere else.

The main exceptions are the French and First Nations who were defeated right here, on the Plains of Abraham (1759) in Quebec and at Batoche (1885), Saskatchewan. It is not "politically correct" to mention these battles and related skirmishes in Canada, but this is no nation of losers. The French have persevered in maintaining their place in cultural life, prosperity and political security, contributing immeasurably to the fabric of the country. First Nations have had an ongoing struggle to survive and to fully participate in Canadian life, but are determined to do so in the present day.

The potential and importance of contributions by First Nations is featured in this book in everything from our manner of consensual government to respecting the environment.

Others came here to win a better life, and did that by accepting and embracing each other in spite of seeming differences. We put "old country" quarrels behind us, like Protestants and Catholics who fought in Ireland but intermarried in Canada. We kept the monarchy, but only as represented by Governors General, a position inherited from New France, and we enshrined ideals from the Napoleonic Code in our Charter of Rights and Freedoms which forbade privileges based on birth. Then we went further through peaceful evolution rather than revolution. We helped establish the Commonwealth, the Francophonie and the International Movement of Indigenous Peoples, and we maintained ties with all the old countries and our American cousins.

We are a nation of winners, keeping the peace at home and abroad, and showing the world how that is done. As our numbers reach toward 40 million, we begin to rival countries like England and France in population, but numbers are not as important to us. Our greatness is found in an ethos of dynamic acceptance, mutual respect and maintaining the peace which defines Canada.

How did we do this despite "western alienation," Atlantic Canada feeling betrayed by Confederation, Québec fearful for its culture, complaints of inattention by Northern Ontario and Labrador, neglect of our North, racism in the Indian Act, immigrants struggling to get both professional certification and their kids into hockey - everybody complaining, except folks in Southern Ontario and its "Golden Horseshoe?" (Sorry, just a Canadian joke.)

How did we create what is the best country in the world in the ways that matter to us? Equally important is the question, "How do we improve it?" Americans have a love-hate relationship with New York, like Brits and French with London and Paris. Canadians feel that way about Toronto, the epicenter of National Policy, though we cheer for the Blue Jays and the Raptors as the only Canadian teams in North American playoffs. We admire the Golden Horseshoe, but we do wish that the rest of us could also find systems which would emulate the good life of Canada's "funnel of prosperity."

Montréal has *joie de vivre* and Vancouver is beautiful, but we are looking for something that all Canadians can share. This book has four themes: what our country looks like, the character of our people, final reconciliation with First Nations, and Canada's place in the world. Some of our stories are thrilling and we revel in their telling; others may be distressing, but need to be acknowledged in this souvenir book so problems can be dealt with. The physical beauty of our country, the mutually respectful and normally tolerant character of our people, and Canada's place in the world are all to be celebrated. The final reconciliation with First Nations is a work in progress in which the sesquicentennial could well be a turning point.

Greetings to all Canadians on the 150th Birthday of Confederation

Foreword by Perry Bellegarde, National Chief, Assembly of First Nations of Canada

On behalf of the First Nations of this land, I greet all Canadians on the sesquicentennial occasion of the confederation which defines the political structure of Canada, one of the greatest countries of the world, at least for most of its citizens.

First Nations join with all Canadians in celebration of the accomplishments of the past, in war and peace. Together we are facing the challenges of the present in which we seek to appreciate each other in a spirit of mutual respect. We rededicate ourselves to a future of justice for all, and success in the worthy goals to which we aspire.

I earlier suggested to Brian Brown that this book should address the desire of many Canadians to finally settle unfulfilled treaty rights, abrogated land claims, and issues related to self-determination which have long prevented First Nations from assuming a happier and more productive place within the fabric of the country whose life we share. I am pleased to see that not only has

he done this, but several of the other contributors have also addressed this concern as a theme of this book and which is perhaps now becoming a priority of the sesquicentennial. First Nations have many friends in our quest for fulfillment of our dreams, part of which is the desire to contribute more to Canada.

In speeches to the Assembly of First Nations and elsewhere I have acknowledged a more positive tone by the current federal government. I have said to Brian that I also observe a change in tone among Canadians as a whole, not everywhere, but widespread nonetheless. We are on the cusp of change in relations between First Nations and all Canadians. Jody Wilson-Raybould, Minister of Justice and Attorney General of Canada, herself a member of a First Nations band, recently observed, "Legitimate and strong Indigenous Nations have already begun to change the way Canada is governed, and for the better."

The next step in this positive rapprochement should be changes in

elementary and high school curricula, as recommended by the recently concluded Truth and Reconciliation Commission. This could enable the next generations of Canadians to be well informed about everything from the visionary treaties which were intended as the basis of our relationships to the negative impact of the residential school system.

One sticking point in moving forward is the Indian Act. Neither First Nations nor Canadians at large can agree on how to replace it short of resolution of the whole range of outstanding issues. I believe that recognition of treaty rights on terms acceptable to First Nations, settlement of land claims on terms acceptable to the courts and political changes leading to self-determination for First Nations, similar to municipalities and provinces, would make the Indian Act redundant. In that case, as I recently told the Assembly of First Nations, "the next 150 years could belong to Indigenous people," and all of Canada will benefit when First Nations become fully engaged.

Meanwhile, arrangements are going forward to bring First Nations housing, education and health care up to Canadian standards through longer term fiscal arrangements. These are foreshadowing settlements in which First Nations become participants in a Canada made whole by their involvement in productive enterprises in every part of this land of rich resources. In a recent speech to the Assembly of First Nations, The Honourable Carolyn Bennett, Minister of Indigenous and *Northern Affairs* for Canada, acknowledged that First Nations are better placed than most to see that such resources are fully developed in a respectful and sustainable manner.

In countries around the world we see oppressed societies and marginalized people reacting violently to the denial of their rights. Britain left the European Union to protect its race, as some of its people imagined. Certain American politicians engage in inflammatory rhetoric to keep Mexicans and Muslims out, and women and African Americans in subordinate places. Such politics of fear and violence have been avoided in Canada for the most part.

French Canada has secured its place as a "nation" within the "country" of Canada. Through the courts and the political process, First Nations intend to be the next to succeed. The myth of a country of two founding nations is about to be exploded by 634 First Nations in over a thousand communities. Together with French and English, and with new "nations" in our midst from all over the world, Canada may be destined to become a model for humanity.

We are "gaining momentum," as I like to say, and the mood of the country seems to support this expectation by First Nations. On their behalf I wish all Canadians a Happy Birthday for the country as a whole.

This foreword material by Perry Bellegarde is drawn from his answers to questions by the author at a press conference on July 12, 2016, quotations from his speech to the Assembly of First Nations on July 13, and editorial notes from an interview with the author on July 14. The publishers express their gratitude to the National Chief for his encouragement of this sesquicentennial project, and to the sterling troupe of political analysts and community observers of the Canadian scene who follow his lead with insightful prefaces to the ensuing five chapters.

Turning Our World Upside Down
with History your teachers never talked about ...
with Geography you've never imagined ...
with new maps to help us shape our relationships as Canadians

"CANADA" – the word is so easy to say that even a child just learning to talk can manage it. Compare it, say, with "The United States of America" or "The United Kingdom of Great Britain and Northern Ireland" or even "The Grand Duchy of Luxembourg," a nation so small you could cross it before you finish saying it. In our 2017 sesquicentennial celebrations, we do well to recognize that our history over the last 150 years – and many more when we count our pre- Confederation story – is never as simple as the name. Though we think of Canada as a "young" country, we are approaching "senior citizen" status. Compared with our 150 years of nationhood, many members of the United Nations are mere youngsters.

Most former European colonies achieved their independence in the 1960s. Sixteen nations attained statehood in 1991 after the Soviet Union collapsed. Even China, Egypt, France, Italy, India and Italy in their present form are younger than Canada. This book will take you through important aspects of our narrative that exist outside the understanding of many Canadians. The result? You will gain an enhanced appreciation of the road – even the detours – by which we've come to this time of celebration.

As important as history is, our geography merits equal attention. In simple terms, we've got a lot of it. Addressing the House of Commons June 18, 1936, Prime Minister Mackenzie King said, "If some countries have too much history, Canada has too much geography." Among the world's 196 countries, only Russia takes up more of the planet's total surface. But as you read this book several closely-related facts may surprise you:

- Though we're big, we're not as big as most Canadians suppose. Even many of our well educated citizens carry with them a lopsided picture of land masses. The reasons for this are revealing. Distance may be the most obvious. A fact of life for people everywhere is that what is closest gets priority attention; with the Trans-Canada Highway ribboning through six time zones and across a mind-boggling 7,820 km coast to coast, much of the country is a long way away. Who dares claim to be fully informed about things Canadian on the other side of the country?

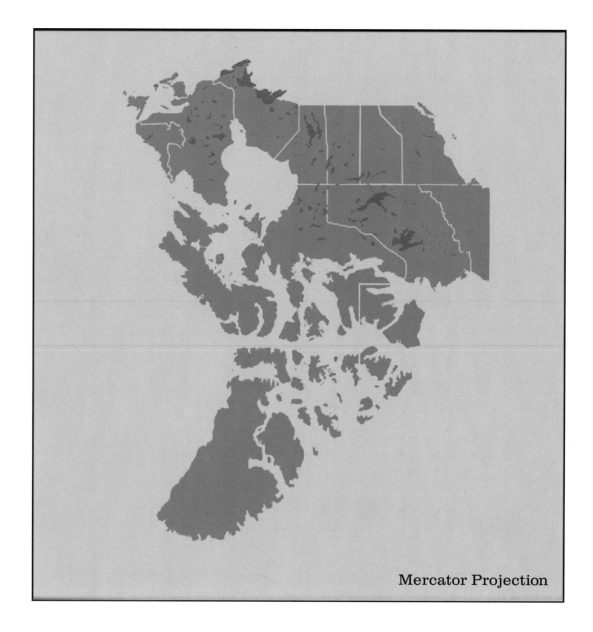

Mercator Projection

Map B: Familiar Mercator Maps of Canada are Distorted, However we View them, Even from the North Pole as Shown Here

16

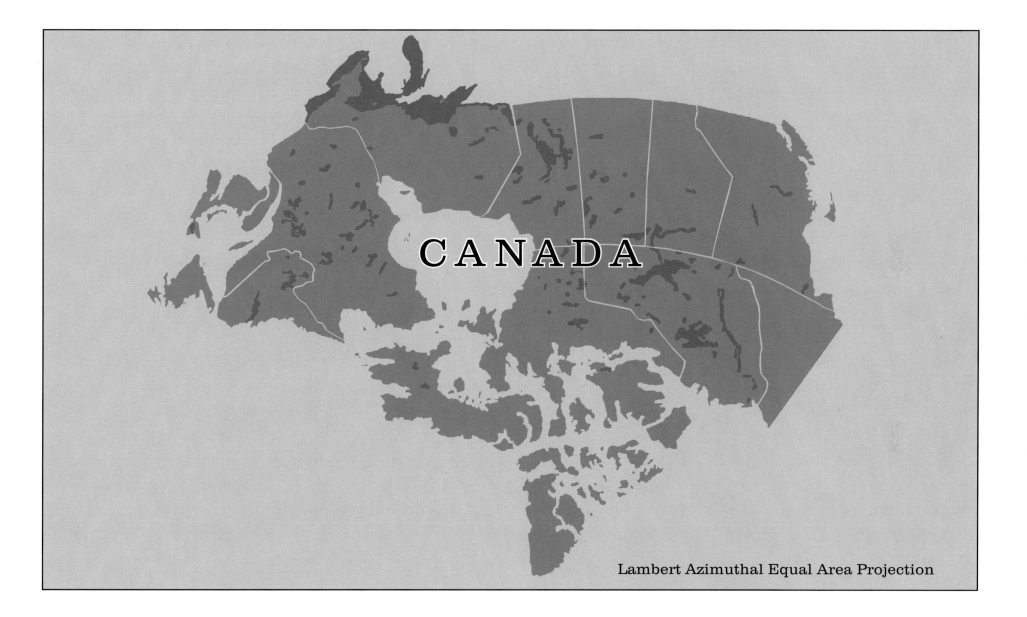

CANADA

Lambert Azimuthal Equal Area Projection

Map C: Newer "Area-Accurate" Maps Show the Correct Shape of the Country from Any Direction; Again Here from North Pole

- Add to this the inescapable fact that for most Canadians what happens "up North" still seems especially remote. This is not just a question of distance, but of latitude: a potato farmer in P.E.I. may feel closer to a wheat grower in Saskatchewan than to a trapper in Labrador only half as far away. With 90 percent of Canadians hugging our southern border, squeezed into a narrow strip less than 200 km deep, often having little family or regular business contact with residents of the North, one begins to understand how it happens that most of the country seems doubly remote to most of its people. Still, that reality of our life together deserves further scrutiny. Is it acceptable that "up North" should carry such different overtones than "out West" or "down East" when we refer to various sections of what is really one country?

- On the other hand, while we as Canadians have more history than we have ever experienced and far more geography than we can fully take in, we cherish expansive feelings about this country of ours.

That may be the key to the future. In the opening chapters of this book Brian Arthur Brown looks at our history. In the middle is the present, and the final two chapters explore our future potential in some depth and sets forth new challenges. Our Sesquicentennial observance will mark not just an affirmation of our past, and not just a self-congratulatory sense of "We're so lucky to be Canadians at a time like this!" but a growing conviction that all of our history and all of our geography combine, becoming an energizing lead-up to the future. Greater things beckon, and we are going to turn the world upside-down to give our readers a more accurate picture of Canada, beginning with our "area- accurate" maps showing Canada from the North Pole.

We said that Canada is big, but not as big as most of us suppose, so since Canadians are not typically in the habit of bragging, why do we exaggerate the size of our country? The main problem is size- distorting maps, no longer used in schools but still ingrained in the minds of most adults. The "Mercator" world map designed in 1569 by Gerhard Kremer became the dominant world image, the one we grew up with, seen here from the North Pole.

When used for navigation the Mercator is ideal, saving the lives of many sailors who might otherwise have been lost at sea. Yet despite serious distortions of land masses, it continues to be used in advertising, as decoration on office walls, on websites, and even a few classrooms.

Like all land in the "high latitudes" – approaching the North Pole – Canada gets super-sizing treatment on the Mercator maps. Compounded with the fact that tropical areas get shrunk to less than actual size, the result is a seriously unbalanced view of the world.

As a corrective measure, in this book we show all areas with mathematical precision on our front cover and on the full sized interior maps of Canada and our neighbours. Our aim is to offer a realistic view of our country at this important milestone of its life.

For yet a different way of looking at the world and understanding it, check out the image on the next page.

On that illustration the various countries are represented not by the extent of their territory but by population. Note how small Canada appears in this regard … and how large Nigeria is! Nigeria appears as the largest country in Africa. It has an estimated population density of 167.5 per square kilometre (compare to Canada's 3 people per sq. km) Its capital, Lagos, is on track to become, in just a couple of decades, the world's largest city. Like Canada, it is a major exporter of oil.

If that does not alter your focus on one of Canada's Commonwealth partners, try this: The Anglican Church of Canada, with its long history (now in its fifth century in what we now call Canada), and with its geographic presence in virtually every corner of the country, counts some 545,000 members in Canada. In an average year, the Anglican Church in Nigeria adds that many and more to its membership rolls. Canadian Anglicans represent 5 percent of the population in Canada; Nigerian Anglicans now exceed 50 percent in their country.

Assuming attitudes of superiority, even before we know all the facts, can be seen as a subtle by-product of our exaggerated size and misleading position on traditional maps. Such attitudes should be replaced by respect for other countries, given a correct appreciation of Canada's place in the world.

A map like this next one may be helpful in fostering such understanding. The Mercator and some other maps mislead simply because they get sizes very wrong, but there are various ways of measurement.

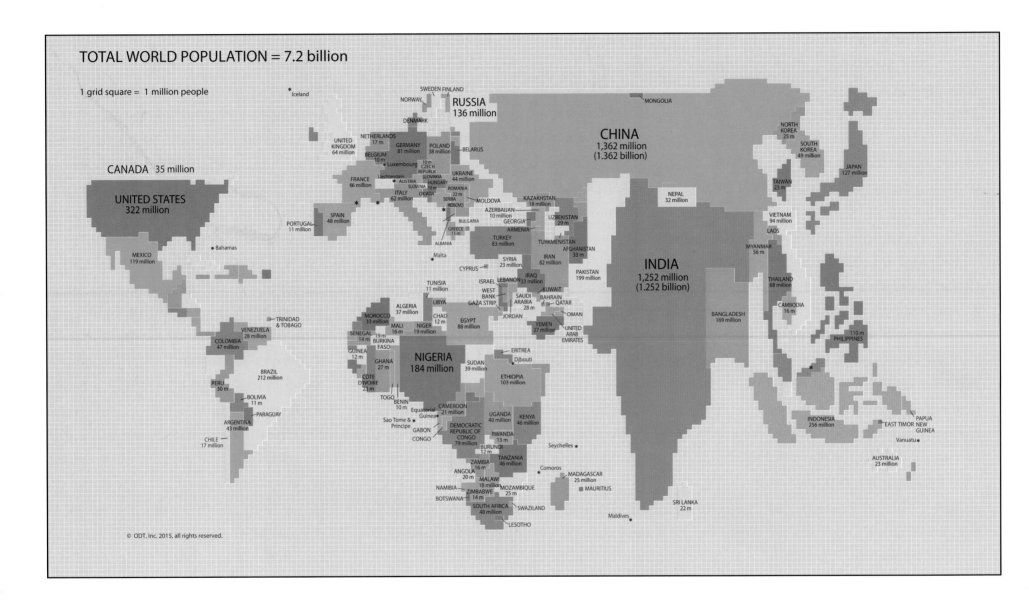

TOTAL WORLD POPULATION = 7.2 billion

1 grid square = 1 million people

CANADA 35 million

UNITED STATES
322 million

MEXICO
119 million

Bahamas

VENEZUELA
28 million

COLOMBIA
47 million

PERU
30 m

BOLIVIA
11 m

PARAGUAY

ARGENTINA
43 million

CHILE
17 million

TRINIDAD
& TOBAGO

BRAZIL
212 million

Iceland

NORWAY

SWEDEN FINLAND

DENMARK

UNITED
KINGDOM
64 million

NETHERLANDS
17 m

BELGIUM
10 m

Luxembourg

FRANCE
66 million

Liechtenstein

PORTUGAL
11 million

SPAIN
48 million

ITALY
62 million

AUSTRIA

SLOVENIA

CROATIA

Malta

RUSSIA
136 million

GERMANY
81 million

POLAND
38 million

10 m
CZECH
REPUBLIC
SLOVAKIA

HUNGARY
10 m

ROMANIA
22 m

SERBIA

KOSOVO

BULGARIA

ALBANIA

GREECE
11 m

BELARUS

UKRAINE
44 million

MOLDOVA

CYPRUS

TUNISIA
11 million

ALGERIA
37 million

LIBYA

MOROCCO
33 million

MALI
16 m

NIGER
19 million

CHAD
12 m

SENEGAL
14 m

GUINEA
12 m

GHANA
27 m

BURKINA
FASO

COTE
D'IVOIRE
23 m

TOGO

BENIN
10 m

NIGERIA
184 million

CAMEROON
21 million

Equatorial
Guinea

Sao Tome &
Principe

GABON

CONGO

AZERBAIJAN
10 million

GEORGIA

ARMENIA

TURKEY
83 million

SYRIA
23 million

LEBANON

ISRAEL

WEST
BANK

GAZA STRIP

JORDAN

EGYPT
88 million

SUDAN
39 million

ERITREA

Djibouti

ETHIOPIA
103 million

UGANDA
40 million

KENYA
46 million

DEMOCRATIC
REPUBLIC
OF CONGO
79 million

RWANDA
13 m

BURUNDI
12 m

TANZANIA
46 million

ZAMBIA
16 m

ANGOLA
20 m

MALAWI
18 million

NAMIBIA

ZIMBABWE
14 m

BOTSWANA

SOUTH AFRICA
48 million

LESOTHO

SWAZILAND

MOZAMBIQUE
25 m

Comoros

Seychelles

MADAGASCAR
25 million

MAURITIUS

Maldives

KAZAKHSTAN
18 million

UZBEKISTAN
29 m

TURKMENISTAN

IRAN
82 million

IRAQ
33 million

KUWAIT

BAHRAIN

QATAR

SAUDI
ARABIA
28 m

YEMEN
27 million

OMAN

UNITED
ARAB
EMIRATES

AFGHANISTAN
33 m

PAKISTAN
199 million

NEPAL
32 million

INDIA
1,252 million
(1.252 billion)

BANGLADESH
169 million

SRI LANKA
22 m

MONGOLIA

CHINA
1,362 million
(1.362 billion)

NORTH
KOREA
25 m

SOUTH
KOREA
49 million

JAPAN
127 million

TAIWAN
23 m

VIETNAM
94 million

LAOS

MYANMAR
56 m

THAILAND
68 million

CAMBODIA
16 m

PHILIPPINES
110 m

INDONESIA
256 million

EAST TIMOR

PAPUA
NEW
GUINEA

Vanuatu

AUSTRALIA
23 million

Map D: The Size of Countries by Population; Just One More Way of Drawing Maps

There is an additional problem when mapmakers are employed by public relations departments to present limited perspectives or even to deliberately misrepresent the truth. For example, Enbridge, a large oil and gas company supplying customers across Canada, sought popular support for extracting crude oil in northern Alberta and shipping it overseas via its proposed Northern Gateway Pipeline through Kitimat, B.C. and from there by supertankers.

They commissioned maps to show the route tankers could take between Kitimat and the open sea, but omitted some features, minimizing the hazards that had to be faced. Biomedical researcher Lori Waters believes that Enbridge may have deliberately falsified their charts, underestimating the grave ecological and human hazards.

On August 15, 2012, the *Ottawa Citizen* gave her story full coverage as part of an urgent discussion in which business, politicians, environmentalists,

First Nations and all Canadians need to participate in the quest for sustainable development. This example shows the importance of true maps for the "true North, strong and free."

Figure 1 below is based on Figure 2 from the Canadian Hydrographic Services, highly regarded in Canada and abroad for the accuracy of their marine studies and charts. It shows Douglas Channel through which tankers would thread their way from Kitimat to the outer coast of British Columbia. Figures 1a and 2a depict the same area with islands removed – a total of 1000 km^2 of land has vanished! – exactly as appears in the Enbridge Northern Gateway ad campaign. Lori Waters suggested that this made the tanker trip seem simple and safe whereas, in reality, moving oil through these islands involves weaving a tanker as long as the Eiffel Tower is tall through 90% angles at the very site of an earlier disastrous spill.

In a comment through Canadian Press carried by the *Vancouver* Sun as recently as

May 5, 2016, Northern Gateway president John Carruthers said the company had made mistakes and is committed to creating stronger partnerships with communities along the proposed route. "From the beginning, Northern Gateway should have done a better job of building relationships with First Nations and Metis communities," Carruthers said in his statement. "Northern Gateway has changed. We are making progress and remain open to further changes. We believe this is the right course of action for Northern Gateway and the right thing to do as Canadians. We know this process requires time and we are committed to getting it right."

False maps and Enbridge's failure to adequately consult First Nations led to rejection of the Northern Gateway Pipeline by the federal government. The announcement on November 29, 2016 went so far as to ban bulk oil tanker traffic through the whole northwestern coast of British Columbia.

Enbridge deleted 1000 km²+ of Douglas Channel Islands from route animation

Figure 1

Figure 1a

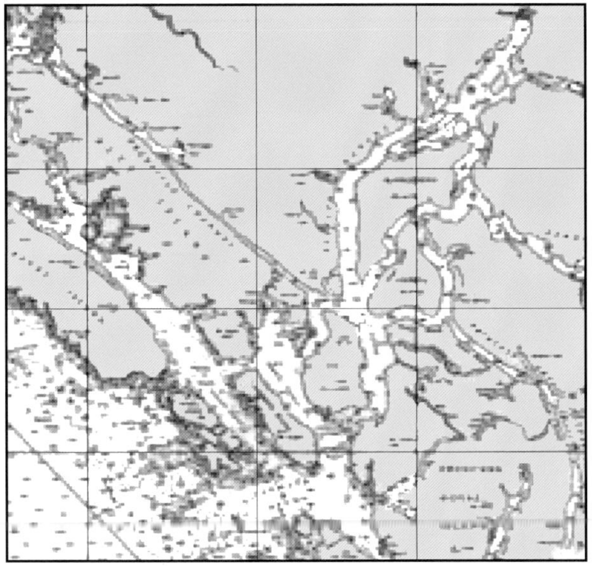

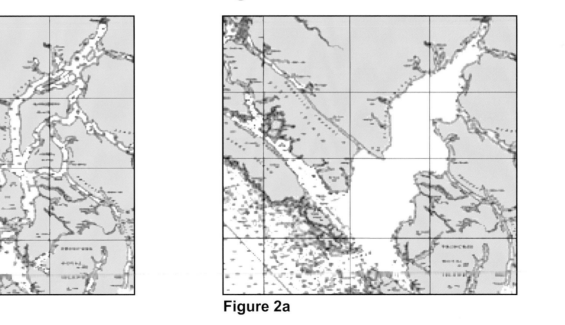

Figure 2

Figure 2a

Map E: Maps Can Be Used for Various Purposes and Even Manipulated to Make a Point or Support a Position

22

Enbridge had learned a valuable lesson, and its more modest Line 3 Pipeline from Alberta to Manitoba and Wisconsin was approved, at the same time as the Kinder Morgan Pipeline got the go-ahead from Alberta to Burnaby in southern BC. These approvals presage the US decision to finally approve the Keystone Pipeline from Alberta to Texas. A typical Canadian consensus may be emerging about restricting shipments of oil by railway, maintaining market share and sustaining employment during the changeover from fossil fuels to renewable energy, encouraged by a carbon tax and other measures.

But if Enbridge used maps designed to suit their own purpose, they were not the first. In the spring of 2001, George W. Bush, then President of the United States, set up an Energy Task Force under the direction of then Vice President Dick Cheney. The names of the members have never been revealed, though Cheney's long association with Halliburton and other American oil companies gives us an idea of the resource personnel available.

They seemed to have given a once-over-lightly to major energy suppliers such as Canada (which exports more oil to the U.S, than any other country), Saudi Arabia, Nigeria and Venezuela. Then the committee appeared to reveal its true purpose by immediately turning its full attention on Iraq where oil supplies were threatened by tensions between Iraq and America since the war in Kuwait, and where false rumors indicated that there were "weapons of mass destructions" in the hands of the Iraqi leader, Saddam Hussein. Though tons of maps of Iraq could have been delivered to them, they chose to create a map of Iraq of their own.

The invasion of Iraq, which conceivably had other lofty motives as well, proceeded with its main objective based on the use of this map showing oil pipelines rather than highways and cities. In other words, "Don't Bomb Here."

Facing that map of Iraq on the next page is another example of how maps can deceive, again found typically in a context of war. In the days before the Second World War, just as Germany was lusting to rearm, a young Austrian named Rupert von Schumacher published this map called *Ein Kleinstaat Bedrohit Deutschland* ("A Minor Country Is Menacing Germany"). The Czech Air Force is depicted flying over Germany, hence threatening the German people. The fact that the Czechs did not actually have such air power capability became irrelevant: the map got wide circulation both inside and beyond Germany.

This map became an effective propaganda tool for Hitler. As a result, when the Nazis invaded the Czech Sudetenland, so many German people believed what they had seen on the map that few objected. The deadliest war in history was on its way, and Canada became completely tangled in a lethal enterprise in which many of our citizens were absent for years, wounded and in many cases killed. World War II was based on this hoax combined with all the other deceptions of the Nazi regime which developed a passion for such maps throughout the war.

A Canadian example also showing how maps can complicate international relations is presented as Map X on page 117. This would be the time to take a careful look at it too.

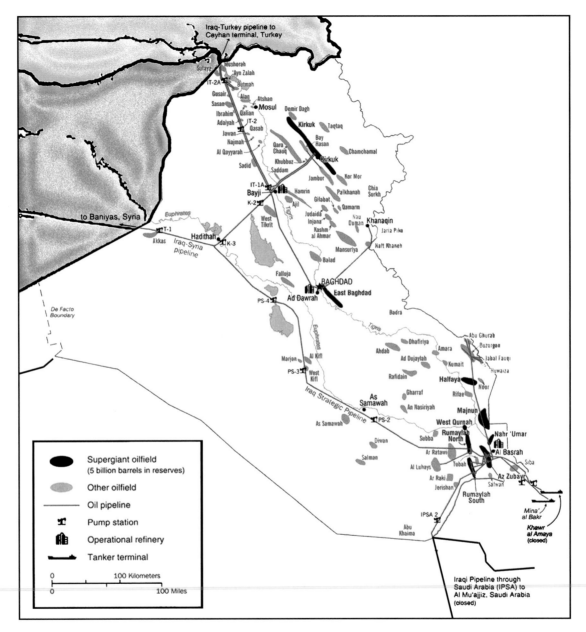

Map F: Iraq Oilfield and Pipeline Map Used by US Military …

the Purpose of the 2003 Invasion was not a Search for Weapons of Mass Destruction

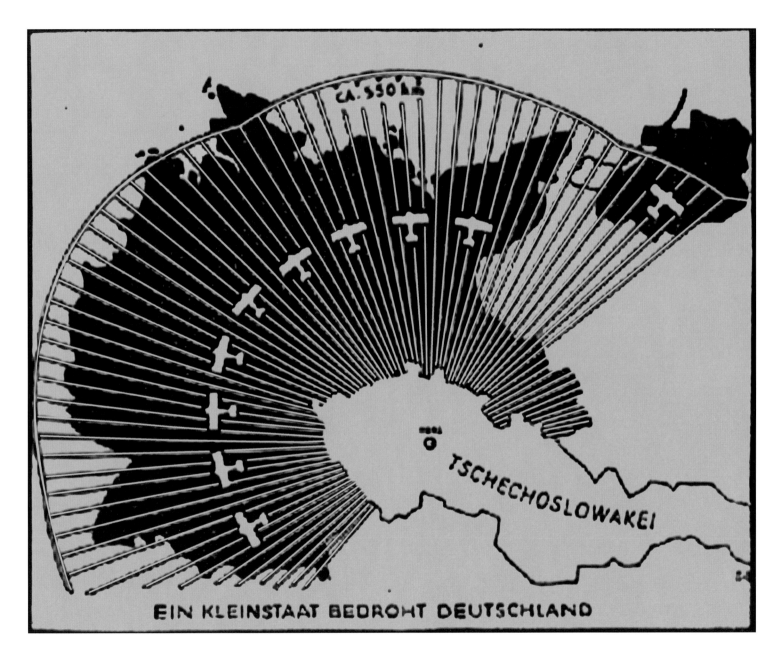

Map G: A Map Published in Germany in 1934 to Create Fear of Czech Bombing (Which Never Happened)

Birthday Presents for Canada

Preface to Chapter One by Elizabeth May, Leader of the Green Party of Canada

Just flip through these pages and get a sense of the breadth and reach of our country. Even seen correctly, we do have a huge land mass, and a relatively small population huddled for the most part in large urban areas that hug our southern border. We are number one in the world for coastline, with over 200,000 km of land that touches three oceans.

As mentioned, Former Prime Minister William Lyon Mackenzie King once quipped, "If some countries have too much history, we have too much geography." In nearly a hundred years since King was first elected prime minister we have added to our history, and also to our geography.

In this the 150th year celebration of our existence as a nation, we are ever more mindful of the far longer history of the Indigenous people of "Turtle Island," as Natives refer to this land. The cultures and nations of this continent that existed long before we came have much to teach us.

The Iroquois Confederacy and its injunction to consider the impact of our decisions to the seventh generation is ever more critical as we face the impact of the climate crisis.

The Indigenous peoples of Canadian First Nations and the Inuit and Métis peoples have all offered those of us from immigrant beginnings in this land – whether recent or multi-generational – much in the form of generosity and patience. Our history is now burdened by the knowledge of the serial abuses and betrayal of promises, treaties and bare faced racism of our past. The 150th birthday for Canada begins with a deep commitment to following a path for truth, justice and reconciliation with Indigenous peoples.

As John Ralston Saul wrote in "A Fair Country," we have absorbed more of Indigenous culture than we generally acknowledge. Our Canadian predisposition to consensus decision-making and a resonance to community over individual identity are both signs that we have learned by osmosis.

We are a product of English and French cultures and of hundreds of tongues spoken here before our arrival. We continue to welcome new peoples with their own traditions and languages and cultures. We are not a country for building walls. Unlike the image from our neighbor to the south of a "melting pot," accepting and absorbing diverse peoples into an amalgam of sameness, we are as former Prime Minister Pierre Trudeau once observed "a mosaic." We form a more beautiful image because we accept and celebrate our differences, even as they are formed from a multitude of pieces into a breathtaking whole.

Let's give our country a present on this 150th birthday. Let's be a fairer country with a fairer voting system. Let's adopt in 2017 a voting system that makes sure that the proportion of seats in Parliament reflect the proportion of votes actually cast for each party.

Let's give our country a birthday present of expanding our national parks system and increasing marine protected areas that do justice to our vast coastline.

Remember to get out and enjoy our national parks in this first year ever when national park admissions have been reduced to zero. 2017 is your one chance to visit our national treasures for free, so get out and explore.

In my beautiful riding of Saanich-Gulf Islands, British Columbia, come for a visit and ferry or kayak through Gulf Islands National Park. Watch pods of our Southern Resident killer whales and Bald Eagles overhead.

Or witness the awe-inspiring sweep of the coastal Cabot Trail through Cape Breton Highlands National Park on our Atlantic Coast. Take VIA Rail from Toronto to Vancouver through Jasper National Park. Get out and hike the glaciers or watch Big Horn sheep from the comfort of the dome car on board.

Let's plan for the next 150 years with a focus on the seventh generation.

Know with confidence that if we invest in our children today, in their education and good health, and in energy systems that give them the promise of a livable world, future generations will honour their ancestors.

It is in our hands to choose that future. Happy Birthday Canada!

Il vous suffira de lire ce texte pour vous imprégner de la grandeur et de la majestuosité de notre pays. Nous avons un territoire immense et une population relativement peu nombreuse, principalement concentrée dans les grandes zones urbaines échelonnées le long de notre frontière sud. Il n'y a pas meilleurs que nous au monde en fait de littoraux, plus de 200 000 kilomètres de terres touchées par trois océans.

Pas étonnant qu'alors qu'il était premier ministre du Canada, William Lyon Mackenzie King ait lancé la boutade « Si certains pays ont trop d'histoire, nous avons trop de géographie. » Mais cela est de moins en moins vrai. Depuis la période où Mackenzie King a quitté ses fonctions de premier premier ministre, il y a 70 ans, notre géographie est restée intacte, mais notre histoire s'est enrichie.

En cette année de célébration de nos 150 ans d'existence en tant que nation, nous sommes plus conscients que jamais de la beaucoup plus longue histoire des peuples autochtones sur cette Île de la Tortue. Nous avons beaucoup à apprendre des cultures et des nations présentes sur ce continent bien avant notre arrivée. Ainsi, le commandement de la Confédération iroquoise de tenir compte des répercussions de nos décisions sur la septième génération après nous est aujourd'hui plus crucial que jamais, alors que sévit la crise des changements climatiques. Les peuples des Premières Nations du Canada, tout comme les Inuits et les Métis, ont tous fait preuve à notre égard, nous immigrants sur cette terre – depuis peu ou depuis plusieurs générations – de beaucoup de générosité et de patience. Notre histoire est maintenant alourdie par la mise au jour des abus, des trahisons systématiques de promesses et de traités, et par les actes de racisme éhontés commis dans le passé.

Le 150ᵉ anniversaire du Canada s'amorce avec le profond engagement d'emprunter la voie de la vérité, de la justice et de la réconciliation avec les peuples autochtones.

Comme l'a écrit John Ralston Saul dans son ouvrage *A Fair Country*, nous sommes davantage imprégnés de culture autochtone que nous ne le reconnaissons généralement. Notre prédisposition en tant que Canadiens à prendre les décisions par consensus et à vouloir faire primer le bien de la collectivité sur celui de l'individu, sont bel et bien des signes que nous avons appris par osmose. Nous sommes le produit de plus de deux cultures fondatrices, anglaise et française. Nous avons été façonnés par l'anglais et le français, mais aussi par les centaines autres langues qui étaient parlées ici avant notre arrivée. Et en ce sens, nous sommes un peuple plus riche. Nous continuons d'accueillir des gens de toutes origines, qui ont leurs propres traditions, langues et cultures.

Offrons un cadeau à notre pays pour son 150e anniversaire. Devenons un pays plus juste, avec un système électoral plus juste. En 2017, adoptons un système électoral qui garantira que la proportion des sièges occupés au Parlement par les députés des différents partis soit représentative de la proportion des votes obtenus par chacun des partis. Offrons en cadeau d'anniversaire à notre pays des mécanismes de conservation de notre réseau de parcs nationaux et d'expansion des aires marines protégées qui rendent justice à l'étendue de nos littoraux.

Allons profiter de nos parcs nationaux en cette première année dans toute l'histoire de notre pays où il n'y aura pas de frais d'admission. En 2017, c'est votre chance unique de visiter nos trésors nationaux gratuitement – alors n'hésitez pas à les explorer! Je vous convie dans ma magnifique circonscription de Saanich- Gulf Islands – vous pourrez y faire du kayak dans le parc national Gulf Islands, y observer des groupes d'épaulards résidents du Sud, et peut-être même des aigles à tête blanche dans l'immensité du ciel. Vous pouvez aussi choisir la route, et prendre le traversier. Ou encore vous diriger vers la côte de l'Atlantique pour rouler sur la sublime piste Cabot qui serpente le long du littoral, dans le parc national des Hautes-Terres-du-Cap- Breton. Ou opter pour VIA Rail à partir de Vancouver, ou encore amorcer votre périple à Toronto, avec comme destination le parc national Jasper, pour faire une randonnée sur les glaciers ou observer les mouflons canadiens dans le confort d'un wagon panoramique. Planifions les 150 prochaines années en pensant à la septième génération qui nous suivra. Ayons la conviction qu'en investissant dans l'avenir de nos enfants aujourd'hui – dans leur éducation et leur santé, et dans des systèmes énergétiques qui leur garantiront un monde meilleur – les générations futures honoreront leurs ancêtres.

Bon anniversaire Canada!

Elizabeth May, Parti Vert du Canada

We need not always criticize the American dream to suggest that there is a Canadian alternative, but perhaps the greatest challenge to Canada's political existence came before confederation in the nineteenth century with what many Americans were calling "Manifest Destiny." This was the idea that Canada was destined to join its revolutionary neighbour.

As it succeeded in doing with parts of Mexico, the United States sponsored invasions to "liberate" Canada: by rebels during the War of Independence, again in the War of 1812 when our militias burned down the White House in retaliation for the US burning the capital of Upper Canada at Niagara-on-the-Lake (though US historians prefer to blame the British, who supplied the officers for that action), and finally by Irish mercenaries financed by the State Department, sent to invade Canada in "Fenian Raids" which followed the US Civil War. These final skirmishes were resolved by early implementation of our "peacekeeping" techniques: massing at the border, pitchforks "at the ready," pushing and shoving, some swearing and spitting, and always standing our ground in military action when finally required.

In the only area with no Fenian incursions, the very existence of British Columbia was threatened politically by an American determination to link the states with Alaska. The slogan of this policy was "Fifty-Four Forty or Fight," referring to expanding the Oregon Territory northward to the 54.40 parallel of latitude to connect with the lower tip of Alaska. We talked our way out of that one in meetings between 1844 and 1846. We may be facing a similar situation in the 21st century as Russia claims the North Pole and most of the Arctic, and our friends to the south challenge Canadian sovereignty over the Northwest Passage. We have survived such challenges before and we can do it again.

America is such a great country that their forces invading Canada were always stunned to realize that nobody here was eager to join in their experiment in nation building. To many Americans Canada is just some more territory of ice and snow between Greenland and Alaska.

They hardly know we exist and many Americans would be shocked to learn that US import-export trade with Canada is close to a trillion dollars per year. This is greater than America's trade with China (always in the news), Mexico (except ours is in balance) and is greater than US trade with Japan, Korea, Germany, United Kingdom and France all combined! Yet daily the American networks report on the value of the yen, the peso, the mark, the franc and the pound with no mention of the Canadian dollar. Reports of the stock markets are given from Tokyo, Hong Kong, Frankfurt, Paris and London, when the real money transfers happen under the radar between New York and Toronto.

Actually Canadians do not mind their invisible relationship with America … we have lots of benefits and few disadvantages in this relationship. But Canadians have difficulty understanding the violence in American society, a nation born with muskets in revolution, weaned on six-gun law in the wild west, growing up through a civil war of unequaled carnage, and living as a violent culture where mass shootings with assault rifles are endemic.

Yet if the USA is not "bombing the hell" out of somebody (to "protect American interests") the US is criticized for not intervening somewhere to help the victims. Moreover, America is the most generous nation in the world in terms of aid and assistance when the fighting is over, or in natural disasters. But the American gun thing is something nobody in the wider world can understand. It has even produced a political ethos of violence in the USA where politicians promise to "fight for you" rather than to represent you, serve you or even to protect your interests.

In the USA every good cause is seen as a "war" on something: drugs, cancer, crime, poverty or whatever. This ethos leads to mass shootings and other violence which results in the highest incarceration rate in the world, at costs to the taxpayer which result in direct reductions in education, healthcare and other public expenditures. While many Americans sleep with guns under their pillows, most Canadians have never even held a handgun and remain, with an incarceration rate at just 10% of the US proportion.

Canadians love Americans, wish them well and pray for them. And who does not enjoy a trip across the border to great hotels, wonderful entertainment and fantastic shopping. We happily concede that America is the world's most "exceptional" nation in military might and in economic activity, occurring through an energetic and creative combination of enterprise and natural endowments.

Meanwhile, little Canada with one tenth the population places well above the USA in health care, education and other lifestyle quotients, according to all rankings by the United Nations and by America's own metric analyses. There is also a balance in Canada between freedom (practically unlimited) and regulation (always on guard) while America struggles to decide which of these is more important.

These two neighbours are remarkable among the nations of the world, but the two visions of the countries are different. It is a cliché in Canada to define the difference as violent revolution vs. peaceful evolution, or more often as "individual values" vs. "community values." The US Constitution defines the goals for American individuals as "life, liberty and the pursuit of happiness;" our Constitution defines the goals for life in Canadian community as "peace, order and good government." Yet America thrives in community and Canadian individuals are as happy as any in the world – two amazingly similar but also very different countries.

Canada's fiftieth anniversary passed unnoticed. In those days, Canada's independence since 1867 was barely recognized beyond the British Empire, of which we were still a part as it became a

Commonwealth of Nations. In 1917 most Canadians and Newfoundlanders were immersed in the First World War, and on July 1 the prime minister was actually vacationing on the Turks and Caicos Islands in the Caribbean.

Out of a population of just over 7,000,000 (the size of today's Toronto GTA) 620,000 Canadians served in that war and we suffered 233,000 casualties (61,000 killed and 172,000 wounded). Few other nations have ever sustained such losses per capita, with even the USA suffering fewer total fatalities than Canada in WWI. Only Newfoundland, then a self-governing colony, matched or exceeded Canada's record, distinguished in The Battle of the Somme and in The Gallipoli Campaign. It may be noted in passing that Canada has never participated in a war to gain territory or to "protect" Canadian "national interests," business or otherwise. Our altruistic military ventures have always been undertaken to protect others.

Canada's debut on the world stage in WWI changed our place in the world.

Our country went through a devastating depression in the thirties and another horrible world war in the forties, but it was in World War I that Canada matured as a nation, as recognized by the 1931 British Statute of Westminster. In it we achieved full independence by peaceful evolution rather than by violent revolution. In the wake of their war efforts, Canada and Australia in particular, as well as New Zealand, the Irish Free State, Newfoundland and South Africa were all internationally recognized as being independent.

We were followed over the next twenty-five years by Ghana, Nigeria, Kenya and other African states and the Asian states of India, Pakistan, Burma, Malaysia and others. Such countries remain related to us in the British Commonwealth of Nations in a manner eventually emulated by former French colonies in L'Organisation Internationale de la Francophonie. These connections partly account for Canada's high standing internationally, and at the United Nations in particular.

Canada's one hundredth anniversary was another matter, with world fair Expo 67 in Montréal and events in every Canadian community. Also significant in the spirit of the era was the establishment of "peacekeeping" as the quintessential definition of Canada's military identity. Of note in concluding that centennial era was a two-volume set of books by Pierre Berton on the building of the railway link which had bound the still vulnerable nation together with bands of steel in the post-confederation era.

The image of peacekeeping still resonates for many Canadians who see it as the proper role of Canada and the United Nations. There are legends about unarmed Canadian soldiers in blue berets standing in a line between murderous armed mobs of, say, Greeks and Turks on the divided island of Cyprus, saying "You can kill each other if you want to but you will have to kill us first to get at each other." This Canadian ethos was established by unarmed North West Mounted Police on western frontiers in peaceful encounters with Aboriginals like Sitting Bull and others from north and south of the border.

External Affairs Minister, later Prime Minister, Lester B. Pearson convinced the United Nations to adopt such techniques in separating Israeli and Egyptian forces in the Sinai to conclude the 1956 Suez War. Pearson was awarded the Nobel Peace Prize for this innovative approach to warfare, an example someone should try again in Gaza, Ukraine, Syria and other places.

The National Dream and *The Last Spike* by Pierre Berton brought Canadians into a romance with their geography, as well as political drama, historical suspense, and patriotic vision. These two volumes told the story of how our founding politicians, Scottish money and Chinese labor built the Canadian Pacific Railway, which then rivaled the Hudson's Bay Company as the entrepreneurial engine of nation building. Pierre Berton put literary flesh on the "sea to sea" east-west vision of Canada, and we hope to do something similar here with the now familiar "sea-to-sea-to-sea" vision, east, west and north.

In 1976 I wrote *Separatism*, which hit the bookstore shelves three days after the election of the Parti Québécois in Québec. It was a best seller in early 1977, at least on the national list then published by the Classic Bookstore chain (now Indigo), partly because no other Canadian writer foresaw that election result. It also sold well because it featured a seventeen-page foreword by my friend, René Lévesque, whose name on the cover was as large as my own – a wise marketing decision.

Lévesque was invited to appear on Jack Webster's popular radio talk show in Vancouver, but he declined and nominated me to speak on his behalf, which I did once a month through that winter. The goal was to explain to alienated westerners that Lévesque's vision of what he called "Sovereignty Association" was "separation if necessary but not necessarily separation" in a new relationship designed to achieve the level of autonomy required for Québec to maintain the status it had originally enjoyed under the British North America Act of 1867.

The BNA Act was our original constitution which contemplated no federal role in education, health care or business regulation, to give a few examples, and no federal income tax. A year after *Separatism* I wrote *The New Confederation*, based on British Columbia's former Premier W.A.C. Bennett's proposal of five "sovereign provinces" (BC & Yukon, the Prairies & Northwest Territories, Ontario, Québec, and the Maritimes & Newfoundland).

This was contrary to our view at present, that more rather than fewer provinces might be better, but Bennett proposed it to satisfy Québec and solve western problems as he saw them. He wrote a generous foreword to my second book as a reply to Lévesque, who countered with an open letter on the back cover and I shuttled between meetings in BC and Québec.

Those were heady days when Ontario feared for the future of Canada, while Maritimers and Westerners scratched their chins about alternatives.

But Lévesque's "threat" combined with the French Language Charter of 1977 in Quebec and a positive response from English Canada to produce a typically Canadian resolution to a crisis which could have resulted in civil war in any other part of the world. Federal initiatives from Trudeau the Elder to Trudeau the Younger spread bilingual services and education across the country to insure the secure integration of French Canada from sea to sea to sea. Meanwhile, governments under Prime Ministers Mulroney and Chretien made reasonable accommodations to Quebec's demands in the spirit of the BNA Act. Finally, under Stephen Harper on Nov 27, 2006, the Parliament of Canada acknowledged that Québec (as the heart and guardian of French Canada) is indeed a "nation" within the united "country" of Canada. Passed nearly unanimously, including support from Le parti Bloc Québécois, the motion read in French, "Cette Chambre reconnaisse que les Québécoises et les Québécois forment une nation au sein d'un Canada uni."

This is now an accepted fact, "notwithstanding" some of the romantic dreams and proposals of more recent separatist politicians, always rejected by the Québec electorate. Now Québec is in to stay and other provinces might sometimes look to *La Belle Provence* to help defend their own independence, as Alberta did in resisting the National Energy Policy of the 1980s.

One size does not fit all; Canada was designed to be a confederation, not a federation. Now another group of "nations" within our confederation insists on being heard in a similar manner. They are not threatening to destroy the country if they do not get their way, but, until similar accommodations are made with First Nations, we will miscarry the destiny inherent in our country's potential … part of the unfinished business of Canada and a foremost aspect of this book.

"First Nations" (French: "Premières Nations") as a legal term has lacked precision until recently. Beginning in the years 2014-2016 The Supreme Court of Canada began to recognize Inuit and Métis along with Indians as First Nations under section 35 of the Constitution Act. However, in historical context the less favoured term "Indian" as well as "Inuit" and "Métis" also remain in use. Aboriginal groups cherish the distinction to an appropriate extent, but enjoy increasing political influence when taken together, representing 6% of the Canadian population now, rather than just 4.5% when Indians alone were considered to be First Nations.

First Nations citizens do not pay federal income tax, pending final settlement of outstanding land claims and long-disregarded treaty rights. For the first fifty years after confederation no Canadians paid income tax, a "temporary measure" introduced by federal finance minister Sir Thomas White in 1917, "for the duration of the war." There are many countries in the world where nobody pays income tax, but where governments are financed by value added taxes like HST, corporate taxes, resource taxes and other measures. Canada's income tax "for the duration of the war" suggests it's been a long war.

It could be argued that a resource rich country like Canada does not need an income tax, and indeed most countries without such a tax tend to be resource rich. Like Canada, Kuwait, Oman, and Bahrain are oil producers, but few are as diversified in other resources. Some like Bermuda, Cayman Islands, The Bahamas and the Turks and Caicos are tourist based and finance traders, and others merely rely on large VAT / HST types of tax. Perhaps the First Nations of Canada got this one right and we should all be relieved of this burden.

Unplanned in this book until its weight became apparent, was the role of religion, prominent in our history, and missed today by media in a country with a dynamic spiritual future, judging by the religious devotion of the majority of new Canadians.

Religion in Canada is never as overtly fervent as in the USA, but neither has it declined in public or private to the extent apparent in many parts of Europe. In the past thirty years weekly attendance at worship has dropped from 54% of people in the USA to 46%, and in Canada from

An Iqaluit Church Under the Midnight Sun

43% down to the current 27%, based on several survey averages. Both figures now approach the longer term historic averages, with just above (USA) and just below (in Canada) one third of the population in church, synagogue, mosque, temple or shrine on most weekends these days. The figures only seem low after an artificial "bubble" following World War II through the 1950s and into the early 1960s. The higher figures remain accurate in the North.

The decline in worship attendance since the artificially inflated figures of the 1950s has been a shock to established churches where costs of operation are up now by 200% while attendance is

down by half. This is ameliorated by rising participation in Pentecostal type churches and high attendance figures in worship at mosques and elsewhere, even in a country where close to a third of the population now claims no active religious affiliation, despite "belief" in God by almost all Canadians.

In Canada over two thirds of people, or at least 25,000,000 citizens profess an active religious affiliation. Of that number two thirds are Catholic, United or Anglican according to the most recent census report. The other third is about equally divided between other Christians and other religions, with some of the smaller groups appearing more dynamically active. With 27% attending worship weekly, this means that nine million people, or ten million if we allow for irregular and occasional attendees, are in church and other worship environments on the weekend. If sports teams could achieve such followings, every Canadian city would have a team in the NHL and we would be seen as a sports-crazy nation. In popular media, the demise of religion in Canada is much exaggerated.

Notre Dame Basilica in Montréal Where Celine Dion Married Rene Angélil in 1994

Leaving by a Side Door of the Basilica Following their Son's Baptism in 2001

The 2016 Funeral of René Angélil was an expression of faith shared with the public

The impact of religion on Canadian life can be seen in peacekeeping preferences (Lester B. Pearson grew up in a United Church manse), shared community care for children and seniors, in art, music and personal morality. It is the egregious exceptions that make the news.

Media reports usually fail to mention that in most years nearly two thirds of refugees are supported by churches and other religious groups (lately including partnerships with government) … more than all other community groups and private sponsorships combined.

Anyone who thinks the wedding of Celine Dion or the funeral of Jean Beliveau at Montréal's Notre Dame Basilica were insincere media circuses does not know this country. However, while in the USA it is a necessity for politicians to advertise their religious devotion, in Canada such a display is regarded as almost a political liability. Yet of thirteen provincial and territorial premieres, six are practicing Catholics, four are active Anglicans, two participate in the life of their United Churches and

one is Pentecostal. It turns out that all political contributors to this book are active participants in congregational life. A survey of the leaders of national political parties reveals that the prime minister is a practicing Catholic, the last leader of the Conservative Party attends Pentecostal services, the leader of the Green Party is an Anglican with theological training, and the only candidate for leadership of the New Democratic Party at the time of publication was a United Church minister, Rev. Cheri DiNovo.

In reference to Canadian history over the last 150 years, it might be simply noted that most schools in frontier society were church sponsored, and almost all Canadian hospitals and universities with roots of a hundred years or more were founded by churches. In spite of mistakes and stumbles by the churches (Indigenous, Jewish and other examples come to mind), without these public initiatives there is little doubt that Canada would be the "banana republic" of the north today, with an uneducated populace and the life expectancy of a "third world" country.

The St. John's-Stevensville United Church, a "country church" straddling the boundary line between Niagara Falls and Fort Erie, was the core of Canada's first Union Church in 1825, in a Canadian ethos which led to the establishment of the United Church one hundred years later as a uniquely Canadian institution.

Founded by Pennsylvania Deutsch farmers from Europe via USA, this

It's Not Notre Dame, but
St. John's-Stevensville United
is a Dynamic Country Church

congregation originally included Lutheran, Mennonite, Reformed (Presbyterian), Evangelical (Methodist), Quaker, Catholic, Gypsy and Jewish members in Canada's first "Union Church," based on an ideal promoted by King Frederick William III of Prussia. This congregation worshipped in German for its first hundred years.

With a massive stone altar of 7.6 metric tonnes and liturgically correct architecture, this church has one of the most beautiful sanctuaries in Canada.

Recalling the flight of many its own members from European conflicts, St. John's-Stevensville United sponsored and welcomed 32 Syrian refugees in 2016, with more to come during the sesquicentennial.

At the same time, the current chair of the Official Board governing this congregation is a First Nations member (a less famous brother of the late Aboriginal folk singing legend, Willie Dunn of Montréal). Its Morningstar Art Gallery (named for the early Morgenstern settler family) features an outstanding collection of "Native art" by Carl Beam and others, and an engaging inukshuk stands at the front door as the now Pan-Canadian symbol of guidance.

Churches are not alone in building an inclusive society in Canada. Many hospitals are now staffed largely by New Canadians, in some cases appearing to be almost 50% visible minority. The business community is becoming increasingly committed to the ideals and the advantages of diversity. Universities and political parties have also been proactive in successful "affirmative actions" which bring their constituencies into alignment with Canadian society. But churches have been to the fore in these regards from the foundations of Métis society until the present day. The sesquicentennial is a time to celebrate what we have been, what we are, and what we are becoming as a country, without lacking in grace about religious life.

In three central chapters of this book we will survey Canada in three centuries: the nineteenth, twentieth and twenty-first centuries of our life as a country. We are appreciative of Canadian glories from the rugged Rockies to Niagara Falls and Peggy's Cove, and we contend that the Inukshuks of the north are ready to guide us to an even greater magnificence in a complete Canada we have never seen.

The map on page one and a pair of maps which follow are perspectives "seen from the North Pole." Others are more traditional orientations from the south, perhaps as seen in imagination from the Skydeck at the 103rd floor of a skyscraper in Chicago. Except for one Mercator map, all our subsequent maps are "area-accurate" renditions.

In the sesquicentennial year we may expect a spate of books on every kind on Canadian trivia "from eh to zed," and the accomplishments of Canadians. Our singers dominate the pop charts north and south of the border, and we make great films in Canada and in Hollywood. In the 2016 Rio Olympics Canadians were awarded 22 medals in our tenth place showing … not bad for a country tied at fortieth in population with Saudi Arabia, which won no medals in spite of its sense of importance. This book is intended as a souvenir of the sesquicentennial, but also going forward with serious purpose. Canadians may be true, north and strong, but not free of self-doubt. I heard readers saying "yes but" to much of the above.

We hope to change that, so there may be some boasting and chest thumping … infrequent for Canadians except on rare occasions. There may also be some "weeping and wailing and gnashing of dentures," over opportunities lost and lingering challenges to be faced. Finally, we present a vision of a great country fulfilling even more of its potential.

In addressing joint houses of Parliament and guests on June 29, 2016, US President Obama said, "America could not wish for a better friend and ally than Canada." He was correct, but Canadians have alternatives to the American dream, as important and famous as that may be.

The book has gone through a fact checking process. While not footnoted in this kind of souvenir publication, almost everything is on the public record. For items which remain unverifiable, or open to opinion, we take refuge in the maxim of Canada's beloved storyteller, Farley Mowat, who opined "I never let the facts stand in the way of the truth," or words to that effect.

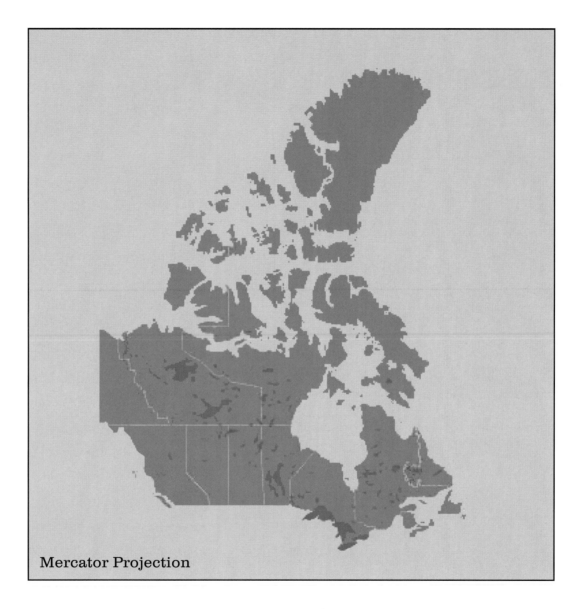

Mercator Projection

Map H: The Distorted Mercator Map of Canada from the Southern Perspective Most Canadians Grew Up With

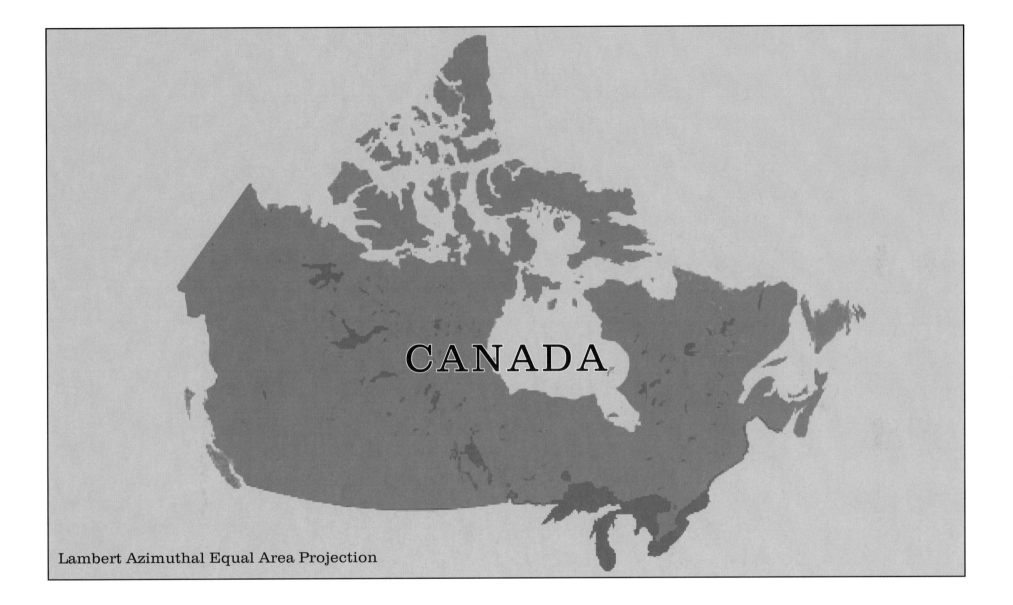

CANADA

Map I: True Shape Area-Accurate of Canada as "Seen" from someplace in the South, Like the Top of the Sears Tower in Chicago

Whose Home and Native land?

Preface to Chapter Two by Ward Kaiser, Curator of Maps

Just to ask Whose Home and Native Land? is to raise issues of who controls what, and so to enter the realm of the 2015 *Report of the Truth and Reconciliation Commission*. These realities are forever interlocked.

Canada now counts two million First Nations citizens. It also includes many citizens with a strong desire to respond positively to *Truth and Reconciliation's* high goals. Until the nation's earliest residents participate fully as equals in our shared space and common life, all of us will be handicapped by the open wounds of our history.

Since so much of First Nations' sense of grievance centres on land claims and treaty rights, a highly effective entry point is to visualize these through maps. A key element of the sesquicentennial could – *should* – be a fresh re-assessment of the size and shape of this land and how it is apportioned. Let's see what Canada really looks like.

Here's a case in point: the author of this book likes to cite my example of our traditional flat maps showing Greenland and Africa as if they were the same size, in utter disregard of the fact that Africa is 14 times as big! Similarly, I take delight when Brown illustrates this habit of some maps in presenting a distorted view, as he compares Canada's far-north Ellesmere Island and Mexico. Maps in common use show Ellesmere three times the size of Mexico, which is a striking reversal of reality on the ground, since Mexico is in fact three times the size of Ellesmere Island. (To see that for yourself, check it on a globe or one of the available "equal area" or "size-accurate" flat maps.)

In short, maps change the way we think. If they can deceive, they can also open up opportunities and realities beyond anything we thought we knew, both here at home and in the wider world. As Canadians we are simultaneously more vulnerable and more fortunate than most other people on the planet. Why? Because we have so *much* geography! Every map can either infect us with false views or liberate us with new and surprising perspectives.

As a result, we need to take our maps, along with our lengthening history and our very impressive geography seriously … and correctly. As you think about questions raised in these pages, you may become part of the answer Canada needs as we collectively map our way through the rest of the 21st century and beyond. We began by turning our country "upside down," enabling us to assess its true size and shape as seen from a new vantage point, the North Pole. This sesquicentennial handbook is offered for you to enjoy, but also for all of us to grow in understanding.

As we celebrate 150 years of nationhood we do well to remind ourselves that this is your history, my history, our personal story – not just the "out-there" history of an abstraction called Canada. Let every "Aha!" moment and every instance of saying, "I never saw it that way before!" bring a fresh smile to your face, a new determination to do even better, and a spring to your step as we walk together through significant scenes of our country's life.

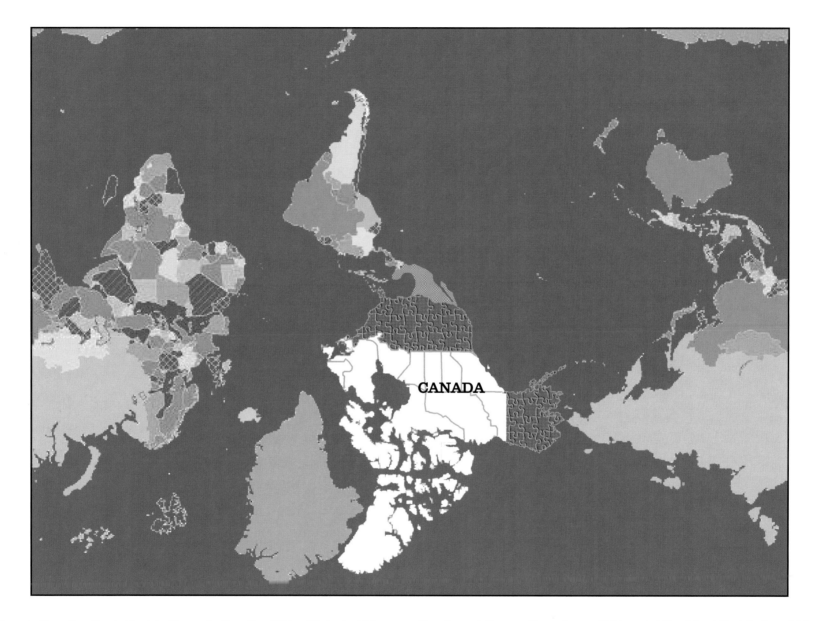

Map J: Turn the Book Upside Down to See the Older Distorted View, an Empty and Snowy Canada, as if Almost 1/5 of the World's Land Mass

Building a Nation in the Wilderness: A Canada Many of Us Have Never Seen

Canadians are celebrating their country and Canada's place in the world as a leader in peaceful co-existence among people. Canada could also be a leader in sustainable development of the resources the world needs. To aspire toward the latter, there are some facts about this land that Canadians need to face, particularly about our First Nations and our North. The Sesquicentennial celebrations give us that opportunity.

To begin with, Canada's north is not quite as large as most people grew up thinking. This is because, as mentioned, the maps we all used until recently distort the global land mass of the world as we look toward the north and south poles. This is especially true for Canada, Greenland and Russia; here is how it works. The earth is a globe, round like a ball. Imagine trying to flatten out a basketball; the centre line remains stable but the top and bottom need to splay out and stretch. Globes of the earth are true maps on which Africa is larger than Greenland which, like Canada, gets vastly stretched on most flat maps.

On some traditional flat maps Greenland and Africa are about the same size, but on any globe you can find, Africa is fourteen times the size of Europe. The ramifications for Canada's north are equally stunning. For example, our Ellesmere Island in the extreme north is not really three times the size of Mexico, as portrayed on most of the maps you have ever seen. The truth is just the reverse; Mexico is three times the size of Ellesmere Island! Two falsehoods here distort reality: one makes our north into a gargantuan ungovernable wasteland, the other trivializes Mexico, a trading partner which has five times our population.

The old maps that used to hang in school classrooms were Mercator Projection maps, and they distort no countries as much as Canada and Russia. Both are large but not even Russia is as enormous as we used to think. Computer generation now makes the production of correct square kilometre maps possible. On these world maps the coastline shapes of countries are not changed but sizes now correspond to actual square kilometres.

The first popular such map was the German *Peters Projection* map, a new perspective introduced to the English speaking world in 1986 by Ward Kaiser, the Canadian responsible for the maps in this exposition. Peters and other "area-accurate" maps are increasingly now used in schools, but few adult Canadians have made the adjustment in thinking about the size and shape of our country.

The image of vast, ungovernable spaces in this "northern colossus" is incorrect. On traditional flat maps of the world, Nunavut appears to be larger than China, but at 1,877,787 sq. km it is not much larger than Québec at 1,542,000 sq. km. Canada's seemingly gargantuan Northwest Territories appear larger than Brazil, but if we ignore its few uninhabited islands, the NWT mainland at 956,000 sq. km. is actually even smaller than Ontario at 1,076,000. sq. km. The significance of this for manageable and sustainable development is tremendous.

This is not to diminish the sense of grandeur of the parts of the country enshrined in paintings by the Group of Seven, but we need to think of Nunavut and the Northwest Territories as the new California and Texas of Canada, with room to grow. Alaska is every bit as large at 1,518,800 sq. km, but more fully developed and with a population of now about a million people, compared to 40,000 in Yukon, 45,000 in NWT and 35,000 in Nunavut.

Like Greenland, Alaska shrinks dramatically when viewed on a globe or "area-accurate" map as compared to Mercator flat maps, but the US has always considered development of Alaska to be manageable, in concert with American Natives. Canada's north is a storehouse of resources the world needs, though our northerners struggle to survive in some communities despite solutions to the challenges of northern living being readily at hand.

Canada has done better than any Arctic country except Denmark in offering self-government to the people of its territories, but the task is not done and we offer too little opportunity for young people to stay on the territories they love, and for others to join in developing the potential of these grand lands.

Among the Arctic countries of the world (Canada, Denmark, the United States, Norway, Sweden, Finland and Russia), Canada is the only one to lack a university within the Arctic Circle.

There are similar issues to be raised with respect to the appropriate development of Northern Québec and Northern Ontario, both of which were taken over by southern neighbours and ruled from distant capitals rather than developing as provincial entities on the model of prairie provinces.

Perhaps the best illustration of how our distorted impression of Canada's size is found in the "National Policy" of our first prime minister. Sir John A. Macdonald persuaded the partner colonies that with such vast spaces it would be only sensible for the outlying regions in the west and the east to send their wheat, lumber and other raw resources to the centre, where Ontario would refine them and sell back the finished products.

Atlantic and Western regions could not be expected to manufacture and ship across the whole land, say newsprint from Halifax to Vancouver or furniture in the opposite direction, so it only makes sense that the original Ontario (shaped like a funnel), should flourish in business. At least that is what Maritimers and Westerners were told by politicians.

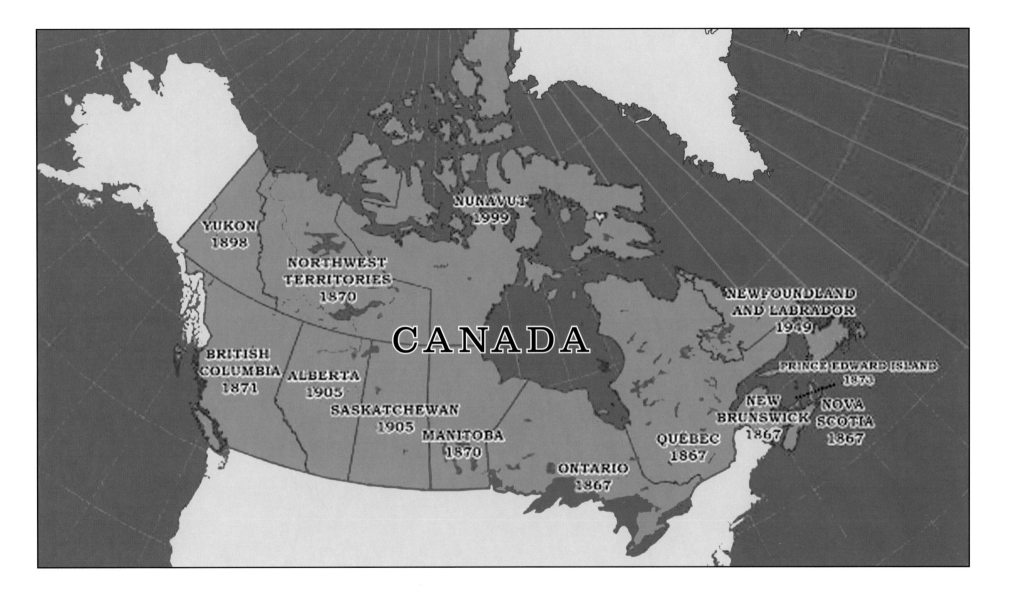

Map K: The Continuous Addition and Evolution of Provincial and Territorial Entities in Canada 1867 - 2017

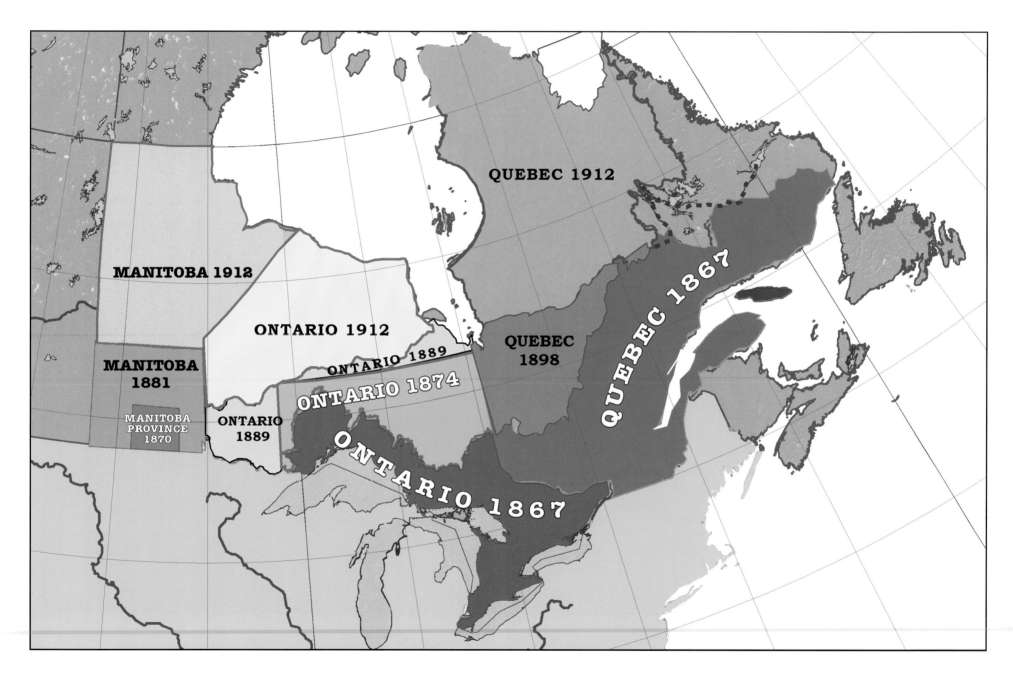

MANITOBA 1912

QUEBEC 1912

ONTARIO 1912

MANITOBA 1881

ONTARIO 1889

ONTARIO 1889

QUEBEC 1898

MANITOBA PROVINCE 1870

ONTARIO 1889

ONTARIO 1874

QUEBEC 1867

ONTARIO 1867

Map L: Instead of Adding New Provinces, Three Central Provinces Tripled in Size, Becoming Super Provinces, Governing from Far Distant Southern Capitals

From this perspective, Kansas would be the thriving centre of the United States while New York and California would never amount to much. However, because it is closer to the equator, the United States has been mapped more correctly. The USA actually has a greater land mass than Canada if we deduct the water surface of Hudson Bay, but the size of their land has never buffaloed the Americans because even old style maps present it as manageable.

By now our readers may be ready to acknowledge that while Russia is larger than Canada, The United States, Brazil, China and Australia are within whiskers of the size of Canada. Our rivals flourish to the extent that they avoid anything like our "National Policy." They prefer to mimic America where Dallas, Los Angeles, Chicago and New York City flourish in outlying areas like Texas, California, Illinois and New York State, not dependent on a centralized structure in Kansas.

Canadian development in the next century is likely to be in the north, but for reasons which are now apparent, Canada may need a new national policy, even though the old one got us this far.

There is no point in complaining that we are underdeveloped because we are so much colder, and therefore underpopulated, since we have the example of Alaska compared to Yukon, Nunavut, the NWT and northern parts of certain provinces. The treeline is moving north and so is opportunity in Canada.

The borders of Canada and its provinces have changed 30 times in the 150 years since the first four provinces joined in confederation. The USA developed its underpopulated frontier areas as "states" in a model Canada might consider to an appropriate degree as "provinces" in our northern territories, and also in northern sections of Ontario, Québec, Newfoundland and Labrador.

There have also been changes in Canada's border with the United States, acquisitions of various territories from Britain, the creation of some additional provinces, and many changes to borders of existing provinces. This has been an ongoing process since the confederation of four small provincial entities.

Between 1867 and the end of the nineteenth century, Canada settled several border disputes which changed exterior boundaries. Disputes with Maine and Washington State were settled in America's favour but on the plus side, Canada acquired the Northwest Territories from Britain in 1870, after holding off American expansion through British Columbia earlier.

In that year a tiny Manitoba became another province, and in 1871 British Columbia itself followed suit, with Prince Edward Island attaining provincial status in 1873 … just the beginning of things to come. The various provinces grew to expand their borders inside Canada. Manitoba expanded in more than one direction in 1881, while the Manitoba-Ontario border changed back and forth several times, 1878-1881-1884. Ontario added seven northern districts between 1889 and 1899. The Yukon became a Canadian territory in 1898, the same year in which Québec's size was doubled northward.

There were more provinces to come in the twentieth century, and there could be more in the twenty-first century, but drawing a line between Canada and an expanding Russia in the north may be the largest issue in years just ahead.

A celebration of our nation's past, present and future may be a perfect opportunity for Canadians to gain a fresh perspective on this land in reference to its actual size as a whole, which tends to overwhelm many of us. For example, how many Canadians realize that had Newfoundland voted to join the United States, as almost happened, Canada would be the third largest country in the world, behind Russia and the USA? Canada is a living organism.

Our maps show three very different Canadas in the 19th, 20th and 21st centuries respectively. But if a previous prime minister thought other countries had too much history and Canada too much geography, he was looking at old Mercator maps of his time which exaggerated our geographic challenges, and we are making history as we go forward even now.

Reference has been made to the role of First Nations majorities and a plurality in one case, in three Territories likely to become Provinces in the next fifty years. We will eventually examine the prospects for First Nations self-government in places like far northern regions of Québec and Ontario also, as they contemplate Territorial status in the next fifty years and who knows what a hundred years from now.

The place to begin a more detailed understanding of the appropriateness of such aspirations is in a region or "district" which never did become either a Territory or Province. Invisible now, this is a place called Keewatin, which should perhaps now again aspire to status as a Territory, and eventually become a Province. It originally included the northern bulge of Ontario, that strange eastern wedge of Manitoba, and a small slice of southern Nunavut. As Canada's Zombie Zone, Keewatin is ready to come back to life as part of the way forward with First Nations becoming full participants in the life of Canada in education, health care, business and cultural activities.

In Canada the tragedy of inadequate and injurious relationships between Aboriginal inhabitants and European settlers was not caused by "Indian wars" as in the USA, but by broken promises and unfulfilled treaty arrangements which became the means whereby cultural domination, economic and political disenfranchisement took place. Two examples from elsewhere in Canada might suffice before we return to our Zombie ghost and its potential resurrection for people in places like old Keewatin's Attawapiskat and Kashechewan communities, so often and so sadly in the news.

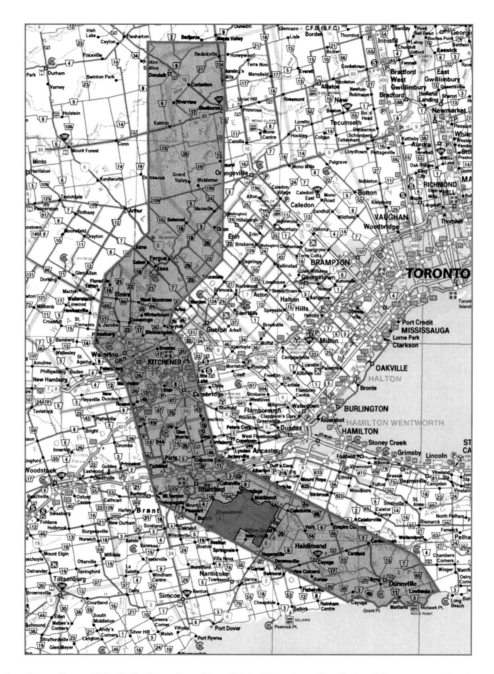

Map M: The Haldimand Tract Proclamation of First Nations Land in 1784, Showing (Red) the "Temporary Settlement" Which Remains to This Day

51

It is sometimes suggested that First Nations were "shunted off" to remote and unproductive lands, but in reality some of the most desirable lands in Canada were negotiated in favour of First Nations but never fulfilled. Even the backwater reserves have turned out to have substantial resources if they could be sustainably developed.

During the American War of Independence, the military and diplomatic leadership of New York Mohawk Chief Joseph Brant (Thayendanegea) is often credited with preventing the sweep of British forces out of North America altogether. He exercised a combination of military prowess on the battlefield and diplomatic skills in meeting with King George III and George Washington and their cabinets.

He met with King George and British authorities in London at the outbreak of the American revolution to warn that the rebels would seize "Indian Territories" at will, offering to fight for the British in return for commensurate support in the matter of territory.

Brant was not a *sachem* or a *sagamore* (national chief or tribal elder), in the Iroquois system of government, but as gifted War Chief he had the support of the clan matrons at the local level and could always deliver well armed and well trained troops to the front. Things did not work out well for the British but Brant covered their retreat.

By this time he was regarded badly by the Americans, much as they regarded general Benedict Arnold, loyal to the legitimate British government but seen as a traitor in the USA. Like Arnold, to whom they also awarded lands in Canada, the British were grateful to the Iroquois. Brant negotiated with Governor Haldimand who issued the following proclamation on behalf of the British crown in 1784.

> Whereas His Majesty having been pleased to direct that in consideration of the early attachment to his cause manifested by the Mohawk Indians, and of the loss of their settlement which they thereby sustained— that a convenient tract of land under his protection should be chosen as a safe and comfortable retreat for them and others of the Six Nations, who have either lost their settlements within the Territory of the American States, or wish to retire from them to the British – I have at the earnest desire of many of these His Majesty's faithful Allies purchased a tract of land from the Indians situated between the Lakes Ontario, Erie and Huron and I do hereby in His Majesty's name authorize and permit the said Mohawk Nation and such others of the Six Nation Indians as wish to settle in that quarter to take possession of and settle upon the Banks of the River commonly called Ours [Ouse] or Grand River, running into Lake Erie, allotting to them for that purpose six miles deep from each side of the river beginning at Lake Erie and extending in that proportion to the head of the said river, which them and their posterity are to enjoy forever.

Brant moved the Six Nations tribal populations into Ontario where this vast international land swap equalled nearly one million acres, equivalent to their previous holdings in the American colonies.

Brant went to London again in 1786 to be hosted and feted by the king, and to confirm these arrangements with the British cabinet. He returned to Canada and journeyed to the now independent USA to oversee the transfer of Indian Territories for which the Natives had now been compensated by treaty in Canada. He addressed the US congress in 1797 to conclude the matter, and to set the tone for an ongoing relationship between Canadian First Nations and their American counterparts, a special relationship with legal implications to this day, as we shall see later in this study.

Meanwhile, the Mohawk, Oneida, Onondaga, Cayuga, Seneca and Tuscarora Nations settled temporarily on tracts in Haldimand County pending surveys and land transfers, while settlers boldly squatted on their territories, next to lands assigned for new immigrant populations. The portion of Ontario assigned for Indian settlement was six miles wide and more than a hundred miles long, now including the cities of Kitchener, Waterloo and Cambridge, surrounding farmlands and the area of Caledonia. The Natives are still awaiting title.

Caledonia has been in the news of late as the site where First Nations protesters finally drew the line on suburban expansion on lands claimed by them in court cases. They have every expectation of finally winning the related court cases, not to regain these lands necessarily, but with appropriate settlements of value equal to the well documented and richly deserved original grants. A figure of ten billion dollars has been suggested in the modern dollar equivalent, adding 1.5 % to Canada's national debt. This seems like a lot of money, except that on the September 17, 2016 eve of publication we note news reports of prime Minister Trudeau announcing that the Global Fund meeting in Montréal raised 13 billon dollars in one day for the worthy objective of combatting infectious diseases, and on the same day CTV reported that 150 billion dollars of laundered money passed through Canadian real estate from abroad in the previous year.

A similar and equally egregious example is the Manitoba Métis Land Claim, which includes much of what is now Winnipeg. Legal title in this instance was negotiated between Métis rebel leader Louis Riel and Prime Minister Sir John A. Macdonald and stands as part of the Manitoba Act. This contract was agreed upon in order to settle the Red River resistance to Confederation and create the new province of Manitoba in 1870, ahead of American expansion in the area.

In 1867 the United States had purchased Alaska from Russia, prompting anxiety in the fledgling Canadian government that the Americans might seek to purchase even larger lands from the Hudson's Bay Company.

Its British-ruled territory, as large as Europe, was known as Rupert's Land after Prince Rupert, a cousin of King Charles II, whose family remained principal shareholders in the Hudson's Bay Company, along with Scottish partners. Sir John A. Macdonald gained British government support to have these lands transferred to Canadian control as our Northwest Territories for £300,000 plus one-twentieth of the fertile areas to be sold by "The Bay" to future settlers.

This area contained the Red River Colony, now known as Winnipeg and environs, which Macdonald was eyeing as a future province in his goal to connect Canada "from sea to sea." This vibrant community had grown out of the Selkirk Scottish settlement to become a harmonious amalgam of First Nations "Indians," a smattering of Europeans (mainly French and English from Québec and Ontario) and a strong majority of Métis.

The latter were by now several generations into a blend of French, Indigenous and Scottish folk, bilingual (functioning well in English but with a French speaking majority), biracial (white and Indian), and bicultural (Protestant and Catholic) in the best future Canadian sense.

This colony was functioning in a semi-autonomous manner identical to Newfoundland, Bermuda and Vancouver Island at that time. However, this society, referred to in official government documents as "Métis" in French and "half-breed" in English, was never consulted about its future in the way Newfoundland and British Columbia would be consulted when invited to join Canada at later dates.

The Métis had been considering a plan to seek "self-rule" on the Bermudan model, as well as both Canadian and American options, but when the decision was taken away from them they simply declared independence. They elected a "provisional government" headed by Louis Riel, who was then given a mandate to negotiate the colony's terms of entry into the Canadian Confederation.

This story is important because what happened in Manitoba shaped Canadian evolution, leaving both Indigenous treaty rights and the position of French Canada to be neglected or betrayed for a hundred years. The 1967 centennial was perhaps among the factors triggering reconsideration in the 1967-2017 post-centennial era, beginning with the question of Québec separation and concluding with the Truth and Reconciliation Commission regarding the First Nations. The sesquicentennial may stand as a milestone in moving to the next stage in both of these matters, essential to the fulfillment of Canada's potential and its destiny.

Manitoba is now appropriately celebrating the glorious province that Scottish, French and English Ontarians built with the inclusion of Ukrainians, Scandinavians, Jews and others. The way forward to final fulfillment including First Nations and Métis is now clear, as we shall see. Ignoring this imperative can only lead to stagnation and decline of this great province, while a positive resolution can be a model for the whole country.

The anticipated inclusion of Manitoba in Confederation nearly went off the rails in 1869 when a new group of white protestant English settlers arrived from Ontario to oppose the legitimacy of the provisional government and to promote a white, English protestant future for Western Canada. Their strident leader, Thomas Scott, was charged with plotting and inciting insurrection against the provisional government, court-marshalled by Riel and executed by firing squad.

After a long standoff between forces of the provisional government and those immediately sent west by the Government of Canada, and lengthy negotiations between Macdonald and Riel in Ottawa, the Red River colonists finally agreed to enter Confederation. The Manitoba Act of 1870 created Manitoba as a province, and granted the Métis title to their properties on the Assiniboine and Red Rivers pending legal registration, with other lands available for distribution to settlers approved by the Canadian government.

At the time, Québec was equal in size to the three English-majority provinces combined and had the largest population of the four, but a minority in parliament. French support in eastern Canada for the French majority Métis society in Manitoba was therefore stymied by a federal administration which was dedicated to the vision of the west as English, protestant and caucasian.

When it entered confederation, Manitoba had a population of just twelve thousand (instructive for us now as we consider the appropriate threshold for provincial status of northern territories). Eighty percent of Manitobans were Métis and a clear majority of them were French speaking. Winnipeg itself had 1,000 residents, mostly Métis business and professional entrepreneurs and their families, who were a majority in bilingual parts of the colony except for the unilingual French district of St. Boniface.

Canada seriously mismanaged its guarantee of Métis rights to their property, a matter only going to final redress in the time of their great-grandchildren during the current sesquicentennial. Immediately after Manitoba entered Confederation, an influx of 30,000 settlers from Ontario overwhelmed the previous inhabitants, driving the population up to 40,000 within a decade, three quarters of whom were white, English and militantly protestant.

Unable to get title to their land, large numbers of Métis packed their machinery and belongings into wagon trains and moved further west to Saskatchewan. There they would flourish briefly, leading eventually to the abortive Northwest Rebellion in 1885 when they failed in the quest for self-government once again. With defeat came the loss of property titles again, pending future agreements … still pending.

Meanwhile as Manitoba became a province of Canada, Riel was elected as a member of Parliament, but fled to the United States as troops arrived in Winnipeg to enforce land distribution and other rights of the new settlers. He would return to try to defend Metis interests in the Northwest Rebellion only to be captured, carted under guard to Regina, tried for treason and executed in 1885.

Riel's statue, one of several in Canada, is now prominent on the grounds of the Manitoba Legislature where he is recognized as the founder of Manitoba. Louis Riel is not officially recognized as a Father of Confederation, though he and Joey Smallwood of Newfoundland are often given that honorary designation.

This all too brief summary should disabuse Canadians of the notion that our country lacks historical drama. The story is not as lengthy or as brutal as the American Civil War or the British War of the Roses. But it is regrettable that many adult Canadians who do not know what our country looks like also do not know the story of how the country took shape in other dimensions.

We have legal challenges which must be faced together if our country is to flourish to its potential, but it is important to realize that not everybody in our history has been racist. Though that has been an undeniable element, the wickedness has been as much structural and systemic as individual or personal.

The first dozen US Presidents held slaves in a cultural and economic system they did not create, but George Washington arranged freedom and other benefits for his slaves in his will, and Thomas Jefferson clearly loved his late wife's black half-sister. He made her his invisible spouse and had children in a second family which reconciled with the first and is a model for America today.

There are just as many examples of this clear distinction between individual understanding and systemic injustice in Canada. One such is the Steinhauer family of German entrepreneurs who provided scholarships to educate The Rev. Henry Bird Steinhauer (born Sowengisik at Rama, Ontario). He became an early Methodist (now United Church) clergyman who insisted on Indigenous application of gospel traditions across the west. Such persons and their descendants have always been capable of self-government. Steinhauer's great-grandson, Ralph Steinhauer, became the first Indigenous Lieutenant Governor of Alberta (and had been an elder in the mainly white Ukrainian Two Hills United Church when this author was the minister there). But in Canada we do not depend on "Lincolnesque" individuals to rehabilitate the situation, not even Peter Lougheed, Alberta's former respected premier, himself of Métis ancestry.

Like First Nations in Canada, African Americans are aware of goodwill among many "whites," but changing the system there required an Abraham Lincoln who was prepared to fight a war against other Americans over slavery, and still the issue is not fully resolved. Unlike the USA, Canada would not look for an individual leader to change the system, but there are currently indications of a more essential communal willingness to address the issues of race in this country. This takes longer, but may produce a truly complete resolution, the like of which our American cousins are still seeking.

The entire First Nations Métis community is testimony to the potential for racial harmony and integration. One of the earliest and more noble attempts to address and support Métis claims was made in 1876 when Manitoba's second Lieutenant Governor arrived to team up with a close friend and business associate who was a prominent Métis leader. They attempted to create a First Nations "District" of Keewatin, in size similar to proposed provinces of

Alberta and Saskatchewan, and similar to the eventually expanded Manitoba.

Alexander Morris had been a law clerk for John A. Macdonald, had a distinguished law career himself, served in Macdonald's cabinet after Confederation, and was tapped for the position of Lieutenant Governor of Manitoba by his mentor. When he arrived there he recognized the fraud being perpetrated upon Métis and First Nations people. He bonded with a leading Métis leader, James McKay, in an effort to redress these wrongs. They were up against the power of the federal Indian Agent, the Hudson Bay factor and the influence of the growing majority of settlers from Ontario whose elected representatives were influential in Ottawa.

In 1855 Morris had published *Canada and her Resources*, which explored the relationship between industry and development. In 1858, he wrote *Nova Britannia* in which he predicted a federation of the British North American colonies, a book which sold 3,000 copies in its first ten days of publication. He also wrote on academic matters and gave leadership leading to the union of the various parts of the Presbyterian Church in Canada (the first and last time that has happened in the world), setting the stage for the eventual United Church of Canada.

In retirement in 1880 Morris wrote *The Treaties of Canada with The Indians of Manitoba and The North-West Territories Including the Negotiations on Which They Were Based, and Other Information Relating Thereto*. This work accomplished little in his day but has become a primary document for land claims in the courts and for government attempts to move on these issues today.

James McKay's father, also named James, was born in Scotland in 1797, a seasoned veteran of the Hudson Bay Company. His mother was Marguerite Gladu, born at Cumberland House in 1808 to a Cree First Nations mother and a French-speaking Métis Catholic father. James' family was mostly Presbyterian but he maintained ties across the spectrum of religion, race and language.

His father commissioned the building of a splendid residence in Red River, from which he sponsored the Arctic exploration expeditions of Dease and Simpson. In time James would follow that example in accompanying and consulting for the British scientific expedition led by Captain John Palliser from St. Lazare, Manitoba to Fort Carlton, northwest of Saskatoon, Saskatchewan.

McKay experienced commercial success in the "old" West of the fur trade and the buffalo hunt, and equal success in the "new" West of agriculture and settlement. He bridged the gaps between different worlds, nomadic and settled, English and French, Protestant and Catholic, Indigenous and Caucasian.

A trader and freighter, his activities also included such enterprises as mail service and road construction. He ran his many business interests from his own beautiful home called Deer Lodge, located in St. James, and was assisted by family members living in nearby Silver Heights, constructed as his father's retirement home.

Mckay was the largest employer in the region with hundreds of wagon caravans shipping goods further west in Canada prior to the railroad, and 150 carts with 450 teamsters travelling annually between Red River and St. Paul, Minnesota.

McKay had served with Riel in the Métis Provisional Government, and functioned as Speaker in the several appointed legislative bodies which succeeded that group which had led Manitoba into Confederation. Such Métis and First Nations leaders as Brant, Steinhauer, McKay and Riel were clearly capable of "self-government" but this was not yet permitted in Manitoba in an era in which the Lieutenant Governor called the tune. By the time democracy became established, the Métis and First Nations were vulnerable minorities, though James McKay was easily elected to the first Manitoba Legislature in 1877.

McKay had bridled under the stalling of Lieutenant Governor Adams Archibald regarding Métis property issues and the failure to enact provisions of the signed treaty rights of the First Nations. White English Protestants poured into the new province with every advantage, including immediate processing of land grants by government officials.

In a vision of what Canada has now become, McKay shared Riel's vision that the west should become the home of a New Ireland, a New Italy, New Scandinavia, New Poland, New Belgium, a New Judea for Jews, space for Germans in a New Bavaria and a refuge for displaced Americans of all sorts. But he did not envision this happening through the displacement of Métis business enterprises and property rights, or the ignoring of agreements made with other First Nations.

When Alexander Morris arrived as the second Lieutenant Governor of Manitoba, McKay made it his business to educate this acting premier and to ally himself with this seemingly powerful individual. In Morris he found a willing and keen partner and they became lifelong friends, visiting the corridors of power in Ottawa, Montréal and Toronto, one a svelte politician in business suits and spats, the other a mountain of a man in buckskin and moccasins.

Yet they found it impossible to turn the tide of influence to get action on the Métis property issues. They also allied themselves to Alexandre-Antonin Taché the first Archbishop of Saint Boniface (Manitoba), to get First Nations Treaties 1 and 2 revised and Treaties 3, 4, 5, and 6 signed, assigning half the land in the province to its original owners. But they were stonewalled again and again in implementation of these acts.

McKay then seeing Métis citizens departing the province, persuaded Morris to decree a legal new territory east of tiny Manitoba and west of embryonic Ontario where no new settlers had yet set foot. But the Métis were already moving west in competition with settlers from Ontario. This unequal contest proved unwise and left the new Keewatin District with an insufficient population base and neither the infrastructure nor the resources to succeed in the transition to a territory and eventually a province.

In Keewatin of 1897 a non- Aboriginal population of less than 100 and 852 "Indians" had settled in Hudson Bay posts. They were complemented by unknown numbers of nomadic "Indian" bands. Organized under a few thousand Métis entrepreneurs, Keewatin might have become a viable First Nations province. Its time had not come, but we revisit Keewatin later in this book since the population has now reached a new critical mass, all First

Nations and ready to control and manage previously undreamed-of resources.

Arguments have been made that First Nations were unready for self-government in the context of the Canadian parliamentary system for a variety of reasons. But Brant, Riel, Steinhauer and McKay were by no means the only First Nations persons equipped to govern. The odds against them had little to do with education, experience or ability. First Nations may have been more sophisticated in relation to the environment then as now. The Iroquois War Council and their subsequent confederacy was erudite, and something of a model for Canada, as referenced by Elizabeth May in quoting John Ralston Saul. But by their exclusion, First Nations went into a century of setbacks.

From the start, a sparse population and seeming lack of resources doomed the notion of the Keewatin district which was intended to become an Indigenous territory and eventually a province, a pattern which came to fruition in nearby Saskatchewan and Alberta with European majorities. So Keewatin was dissolved by blending parts of it into Ontario and Manitoba, and back into the Northwest Territories where a portion remains today in Nunavut.

The Nunavut model, still a work in progress more than a hundred years later, did give self-government and resource control to First Nations, finally succeeding as an alternative to the racist Indian Act. To this day First Nations people decry that Act, but cannot agree on a formula for replacement short of self-government. This appears to be destined to become the new normal in future years, transforming First Nations and renovating Canada in a fundamental manner not yet recognized by many Canadians.

Meanwhile, as temperatures rise with global warming, Hudson Bay will become "The Baltic Sea of North America." This will be perhaps the most visible result of climate change in Canada, but largely unrecognized to date. No longer at the outer fringe of populated areas of the country, Hudson Bay is set to become a new hub of the north in the next hundred years, surrounded then by three new provinces in Northern Ontario, Northern Quebec and Nunavut. This will be our very own "Candinavia," similar to the Scandinavia of Norway, Sweden, Finland and other Arctic entities at the same Baltic latitude in Europe. The big question is whether or not the rest of Canada get its relations with First Nations right this time, possibly leading to their full participation in the sustainable development of one of the wealthiest parts of the world in terms of both human and natural resources.

First Nations control of their own resources is obviously far preferable to the patronizing bestowal of larger and larger grants of money from the federal government. Canadians feel despair at the mention of communities like Attawapiskat and Kashechewan in Northern Ontario where people wish to live on the land their ancestors had managed for 20,000 years. They know that this land, considered god-forsaken by other Canadians, does have the resources to sustain the First Nations there if they could get their hands on those assets … resources which they could develop in a harmony between nature and human community, seen as an ideal in the twenty-first century.

Too many First Nations citizens migrate to the cities in a swath through the portion of Northern Ontario in a line from North Bay to Winnipeg. There they barely function in a disorientation similar to Afro- Americans in urban ghettos who have needed several generations to recover from the trauma of slavery before one of them was ready to become President. In the NWT, Premier Bob McLeod is Métis and in Nunavut Premier Peter Tapyuna is Inuit. We are not there yet nationally in Canada, but we may have a First nations prime minister before our bicentennial in 2067.

In 2016 the federal Government of Canada agreed to finally settle the 146-year-old Métis claim, following a 2013 landmark decision by the Supreme Court of Canada which affirmed "the Manitoba Act of 1870," which brought Manitoba into Confederation. That act had recognized Métis Aboriginal rights by way of their Indian ancestry, and granted 1.4 million acres of land "for the benefit of families of half-breed residents."

On May 27, 2016, federal Minister of Indigenous and Northern Affairs Carolyn Bennett signed a memorandum of understanding with Manitoba's Métis which she described as "the government's commitment to finally honour a promise made by Sir John A. Macdonald to distribute 5,565 square kilometres of land, including what later became modern-day Winnipeg, to the Métis."

Again, there is no indication that the Métis may take over Winnipeg, though huge swathes of Crown Land may be transferred and the settlement of the claim involves the several billions of dollars needed for the Métis educational, health, business and other enterprises. This debt has been on our books for too long, equivalent to perhaps 0.5% of Canada's national debt which was rung up on projects no less worthy.

Similar but smaller claims have already been successfully litigated in court and followed by legislation in Kanesatake, adjoining Montréal, and Kitsilano in Vancouver. These successes are leading the way toward settlement of several hundred claims now before the courts. There is now a push to settle all these matters in a manner which holds the potential to bring First Nations communities up to the living standards of other Canadians. This, of course, also requires the abolition of the Indian Act and the "granting" of self-government to First Nations in managing their affairs as municipalities, territories or even as provinces in certain cases.

Canadians are still digesting the report of the seven-year Truth and Reconciliation Commission (2008 – 2015) examining the impact of the residential school system on Native children and First Nations communities, which toured the country with a panel under Justice Murray Sinclair, Associate Chief Justice of Manitoba, himself a highly respected Indigenous judge. The primary focus was on schools run by Roman Catholic, Anglican, United and Presbyterian Churches with government funding from 1870 until 1996.

What Canadians should realize is that the Indian Act, the abrogation of treaty rights and the residential school system, impacted the Canadian First Nations in ways similar to the way slavery impacted African Americans. That grave matter is our neighbour's affair, and we Canadians have smugly regarded ourselves as well-informed and above all that.

The enduring impact is not limited to merely the horrors of sexual abuse, corporal punishment, absence from family connections for years on end and untimely deaths of thousands of children, often unreported, at residential schools. The more profound impact has to do with self respect and personal identity.

The African slaves arrived in America as Muslims and lost their religion. They spoke a variety of languages but were separated culturally and lost their languages. People who thus lose their identity quickly become disabled and disenfranchised in a manner which takes generations to overcome, as we see in American ghetto communities. US First Lady Michelle Obama's grandfather was born to former slaves, and while she and some others have recovered from the devastating communal experience, many are still working through the aftermath of what are relatively recent experiences, with both encouragement and resistance from the majority community. The African

American community makes up 10% of the population of the United States, and the issue of race is a fact of American life.

Canada is at a similar place with First Nations, though according to the 2016 census they make up 6% of our population. However, census figures indicate that indigenous people make up 22% of Labrador's population, 18% in Manitoba and 20% in Saskatchewan, well above minority figures in most specific US states. Our country has continued to accommodate New Canadians from all over the world, once they pay their dues. Québec has found the strength within to insist upon the original standing of French culture and business in Canada. The agenda of the country for the next fifty years must be a similar reconciliation with First Nations.

These are the people who have welcomed others to these shores since the time of Jacques Cartier. In many cases they accepted Samuel de Champlain's proposal that "Our sons shall wed your daughters and henceforth we shall be one people." They fought alongside the rest

of us through three invasions from the south and two world wars. They accepted treaty agreements to develop the land and its resources. Failure to make this next accommodation would see Canada continue to fall short of its potential for First Nations and for the country as a whole.

The Truth and Reconciliation Commission in Canada brought forward a report which has been well received by First Nations, federal and provincial governments, the churches, educators, media and the nation as a whole. There is a consensual desire to see its myriad important recommendations concerning conditions in First Nations communities implemented.

It is time to move beyond the Truth and Reconciliation Report's remedies for past and present problems. The next step is the honoring of hundreds of treaty provisions and land claims now before the courts. This must be followed in the next fifty to one hundred years by the evolution of self-government in First Nation majority areas, with municipal, territorial or provincial status, depending on the situation.

A national survey reported by Canadian Press on June 8, 2016 found that three-quarters of non-Aboriginal Canadians believe the residential school system harmed Aboriginal people, yet just 5% believe the federal government should pay compensation to try to heal those wounds.

The Environics Institute telephone survey of 2,001 non-Aboriginal adults from across the country conducted in January and February, 2016, also found 66 per cent of Canadians are learning about Indigenous peoples and their issues, but 10 per cent still believe Indigenous People get "special treatment" from governments.

National Chief Perry Bellegarde released a statement on the survey, saying that the results show the views of non-Aboriginal Canadians are still tainted by negative stereotypes. "If you want reconciliation, you need to make space in your mind, your heart and spirit to get rid of the misconceptions you have about Indigenous Peoples," he said. "The stereotype that Indigenous Peoples are dumb, stupid, lazy, drunk and on welfare — put that aside."

What Bellegarde hopes for is laudable, but those who believe that the federal government has no further responsibility to First Nations are missing the point. Any "special treatment" Indigenous people receive from government is in the form of temporary band-aids to mask the miscarrying of legal treaty obligations and the necessity for First Nations to govern themselves, with resource management responsibilities commensurate with treaty provisions. These issues are systemic not attitudinal.

New personal attitudes may be appropriate but they will not come about through mere goodwill and they will not change the systems. Other Canadians will have respect for First Nations when they see them taking care of business for themselves, and this they are able and ready to do when the systemic playing field becomes level at last.

This book has several themes, from the physical shape of Canada and the peaceful character of its people, living in harmony and mutual respect, to Canada's place in the world. But if the 1967 centennial of confederation is remembered for Expo 67, it is our hope that the sesquicentennial may be remembered for the progress made in Truth and Reconciliation. We have referenced the disregarded treaty rights, the stalled land claims, the necessity of First Nations self- government and the cultural devastation of the residential school system. The final matter requiring urgent redress is the matter of *Missing and Murdered Indigenous Women*, to quote the title of a federal commission named on August 3, 2016 to work on this matter through the sesquicentennial year and to report with recommendations shortly thereafter.

The problem goes back much further, but came into public consciousness in 2004 with the release of a government survey showing that Indigenous women report rates of violence, including domestic violence and sexual assault, 3.5 times higher than non-Indigenous women. Canadians were confronted later that year by an Amnesty International assessment, *Stolen Sisters: A Human Rights Response to Discrimination and Violence against Indigenous Women in Canada* which documented some of the underlying causes of violence against Indigenous women carried out by both Indigenous and non-Indigenous men. As the report showed, widespread and entrenched racism, poverty and marginalization are critical factors exposing Indigenous women to a heightened risk of violence, while denying them adequate protection by police and government services.

Until those reports, when other Canadians would hear of Indigenous women gone missing or on the receiving end of "foul play," the response was too often "What do they expect when they insist on participating in high-risk lifestyles?" The reports began the process of awareness of the problems listed above. What the Indigenous women have been facing is more systemic than personal, though the brunt of the burden fell on unfortunate individuals who lacked other real alternatives. Studies suggest that assaults against Indigenous women are not only more frequent, they are also particularly brutal. According to another government survey, young First Nations women are five times more likely than other women to die as a result of violence.

The impact on children in residential schools and female victims of violence has profound effects on their families and communities, but like treaty rights, land claims and self-government, the solutions in such cases begins not with women behaving differently as individuals, important as that may be. Progress toward redress will only begin with realization that it is systemic injustice which exacerbates the problems faced by First Nations and distinguishes them from other Canadians.

Despite Canada's pride in the RCMP and respect for the work of all our police forces, it has been painful to watch CBC and CTV news reports as recently as 2015 and 2016 indicating strained relations between the police and First Nations. While in the USA it is young black males who need to fear rogue racist police, in Canada that fear is apparently felt more by young indigenous women who have testified to rape, exploitation and violence.

It has taken twelve years to move from awareness of the problem to the setting up of a commission to recommend action on *Missing and Murdered Indigenous Women*. Meanwhile, an update to the 2004 *Stolen Sisters* report highlights the continuing marginalization and inequality experienced by Indigenous women in five areas:

1) Racism and misogyny in perpetuating violence against Indigenous women;
2) Disparities in Indigenous women's economic, social, political & cultural rights;
3) Continued disruption caused by removal of children from Indigenous families;
4) The disproportionately high number of Indigenous women in Canadian prisons
5) Inadequate police response to violence against Indigenous women.

To quote the terms of the commission of inquiry, "The scale and severity of the human rights violations faced by Indigenous women requires a coordinated and comprehensive national response that addresses the social and economic factors that place Indigenous women at heightened risk of violence." Justice Marion Buller, herself an Indigenous lawyer from British Columbia, and four other distinguished Indigenous jurists have been tasked to bring this national tragedy to an end. To succeed they will need to engage the interest and the support of all Canadians. The inquiry began on Sept. 1, 2016 and will run until Dec. 31, 2018 with hearings, by coincidence or design, running through the sesquicentennial year.

Canadian Images from Poppies to Terry Fox Runs

Preface to Chapter Three by The Hon. Rob Nicholson, MP for Niagara Falls

Brian Arthur Brown has been writing insightfully about Canada for forty years, and Ward Kaiser has been a distinguished Canadian participant in international mapmaking projects to assist people to see themselves and each other accurately. I commend them for this engaging presentation to celebrate the one hundred and fiftieth anniversary of this great land in 2017.

In addition to expressing my personal loyalty and love for our country, having served as Minister of Foreign Affairs for Canada in the run up to the sesquicentennial, I have been asked to tell you something of the ways in which people around the world appreciate what Canada has done and is doing, and how Canada influences their thinking.

For example, I was recently in the Netherlands for the seventieth anniversary of the liberation of that country by Canadian troops in the Second World War, and the grateful atmosphere among its citizens was such that one would think they had been liberated by Canada just 7 months ago, rather than 70 years ago.

In a recent visit to the Ukraine I noticed that people wore poppies on their Remembrance Day, and when I asked about it I was told, "We have just begun the tradition, something we picked up from Canada."

In a recent conversation with the Foreign Minister of the United Arab Emirates, I learned that he had just completed the Terry Fox Run. I asked if he had been in Canada, and he replied, "Oh no, we have the Terry Fox Run in Dubai. We had 20,000 participants."

Canada's influence in the world is actually growing in significant areas like finance, trade and security. The Eastern European countries of NATO appreciate our military presence there in this era of Russian expansionism, and in Kiev they have expressed gratitude for the realization that we intend to stand by Ukraine for the long term.

Israel too has acknowledged that in the midst of their ongoing vulnerability in that volatile part of the world, they know that Canada is committed to their security.

I recently met with the Foreign Minister of Iraq in Québec City, where Canada convened a conference on important steps in Middle East conflicts and, while solutions are not easy, Iraq and all the other players value the input and recognize the commitment of Canada in resolving things long term.

Part of this comes out of the success story of the ethnic mix in Canada itself, in a harmony which is a model for the world. I have complete confidence that Québec has worked through its issues and will remain part of the Canada which it was a key partner in creating as a country. The advancement of our First Nations must remain a priority for our federal government and for all future governments at every level, keeping in mind that there could not have been a Canada without treaties, military alliances, and their loyalty and participation two hundred years ago in the nation building era prior to confederation.

Canada faces challenges in the future with respect to climate change, sustainable development of our resources, and expansion of our stewardship of the north. First Nations may have a role in these areas too, but every Canadian must share in responsibility for mature progress in these regards.

Russia has planted a flag at the North Pole, a location I have always regarded as Canadian. Discussion of these boundaries and the related resources is currently before the United Nations. Canada and Denmark have provided models for resolution of such questions in the boundary areas between Baffin Island and Greenland.

Canada will maintain its sovereignty over parts of the north and the Arctic where we have people living, regular patrols by the Canadian Rangers, a recognized governmental presence, and even federal cabinet meetings on tours in which I have often participated.

If the Russians have any thoughts of moving into our sovereign territory, as they have done in Crimea and Western Ukraine, all I can say is that they would be wise to think again.

Canada's past has been glorious. Our present is the envy of the world. Our future is secure.

Happy Birthday, Canada!

Expanding Canada, Turning Ontario and Québec into Provincial Empires, and First Nations Gone Missing

People think Canada's seventh prime minister, Sir Wilfrid Laurier, said "The 20th century belongs to Canada." What he actually said in 1904 was: "The 19th century was the century of the United States. I think we can claim that it is Canada that shall fill the 20th century." Laurier's optimism came on the eve of Alberta and Saskatchewan entering confederation shortly after Yukon became a Territory, also on his watch.

We did well in the 20th century. Canadians do not need to be first in wealth or power, but for much of the 1990s, for example, Canada did top the United Nations' Human Development Index, and we are often number one or ranked highly in surveys of lifestyle, healthcare, happiness, and other categories.

The 20th century did belong to the USA in areas from sports and war to popular culture and entrepreneurial energy, despite vicious but futile attempts at world domination by Germany and Russia. In terms of power, economics and influence, China is already laying claim to the 21st century, and the 22nd century may yet belong to India. But with careful management, Canada can rival the Scandinavian "valhallas" of education, healthcare, peacekeeping and other measures of happiness in which they alone equal our performance, followed in some instances by Australia, New Zealand, Switzerland and Japan.

In the 20th century Canada was blessed in achieving territorial integrity "from sea, to sea, to sea," with the accession of Alberta and Saskatchewan at the beginning of the century, the joining by Newfoundland and Labrador mid-century, and by the evolution of Nunavut to territorial status at the end of the century. In that recent century Ontario and Québec doubled in size, again, with borders pushing north, and each is larger now than any European country. Canada survived Québec's flirtation with separation, though among ten provinces only Ontario has never elected a provincial government pledging to exit confederation … except Newfoundland, which first voted against Canada before voting to join.

In social development Canadians are fond of pointing out that progressive legislation in this country preceded similar developments south of the border by decades, from peacekeeping to multiculturalism, and from healthcare to same-gender marriage, as well as anti-discrimination laws on other fronts.

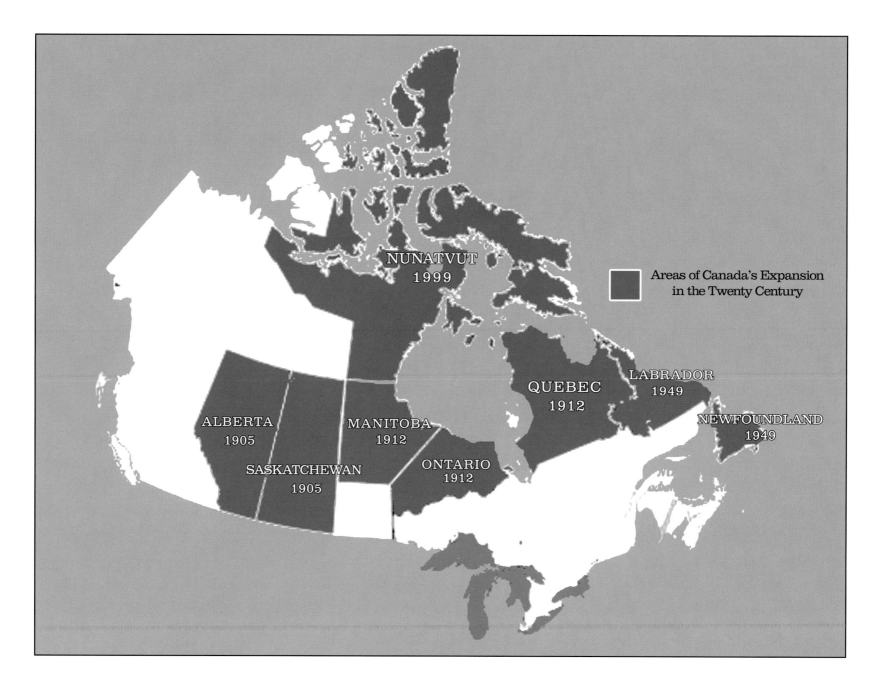

Map N: After 19ᵗʰ Century Beginnings, the 20ᵗʰ Century Saw Eight Major Additions to Canada. What Will the 21ˢᵗ Century Bring?

Canada accepted "draft dodgers" resisting a war in Vietnam which America itself eventually rejected. In that instance 25,000 young American professionals arrived in a twentieth century parallel to the earlier underground railway in which 30,000 refugees from slavery were able to flee. Both groups followed trails established earlier by 45,000 United Empire Loyalist refugees, even before Confederation. All of these Americans were "seeking a better country," followed the Canadian dream and contributed much to the fabric of this land.

Notwithstanding the fact that Canada had no "Indian Wars" as such, Canada's history and our current relationship with our original Aboriginal peoples remains perhaps the greatest blot on the character and reputation of this country. This is a serious impediment to full development of the potential of both the majority of our citizens and this under-achieving minority, restricted in many cases to seemingly remote wastelands.

First Nations self-government and their role in management of resources increasingly identified in those "remote wastelands" represent a double helix of the DNA of Canada, which may be a key to the future of us all. Accordingly, we find ourselves returning to these themes time and again in this summary of the greatness of our country and the challenges we face.

The United States still struggles to overcome the disenfranchisement and disorientation of one minority in particular, though Natives and Hispanics too have their stories of exclusion in America. The fulfillment of the national dream in Canada has been delayed by roadblocks preventing full participation by two large and significant minorities, the French "nation" and the First Nations, even as we continue together in one "country."

French Canada has had a role in Canadian political leadership from the beginning but, for example, never a federal finance minister (the seat of real power) until Jean Chrétien was appointed immediately after a provincial government threatening separation drew such matters to everyone's attention.

Similar examples of restrictions on First Nations in the halls of power are simply far too numerous to list. To avoid arrest after his election to the Parliament of Canada, Louis Riel himself had to sneak into the House of Commons in Ottawa one night to sign the register before fleeing to the USA for safety. Parliament would then be deprived of elected persons of Indigenous ancestry until Len Marchand became parliamentary secretary in 1968, then cabinet minister in the first Trudeau administration.

Redress in the first instance of French Canada has come; there should be excitement in the land in this sesquicentennial era as reconciliation with First Nations becomes increasingly recognized as a national priority. This book is intended to put this matter on the national agenda during the sesquicentennial year, but well begun is only half done and this priority will occupy our attention for years to come.

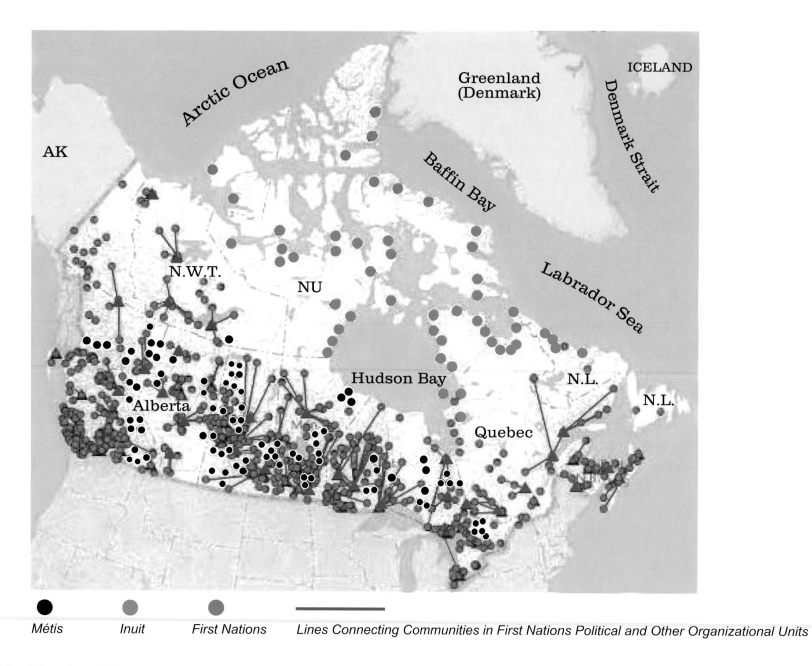

Métis   **Inuit**   **First Nations**   Lines Connecting Communities in First Nations Political and Other Organizational Units

Map O: More Than Two Million Indigenous Citizens in a Thousand Communities, First Nations Status and Non-Status Indian, Métis and Inuit in a New Canada

Inherent weaknesses in the reservation system, flaws in the "Indian Act," failure of non-Indigenous Canadians to live up to treaty obligations, the horrors of the residential schools, missing and murdered Aboriginal women, personal and familial debilitation in the aftermath of such experiences all need to be addressed and dealt with. According to the 2016 census, there are now more than two million First Nation Canadians of "Status Indian," non- status, Métis and Inuit ancestry. A majority of these remain largely outside the robust sense of well being enjoyed by most other citizens of Canada.

The recent acknowledgment by the Truth and Reconciliation Commission of the shocking legacy of residential schools opened the eyes of many Canadians. Others have begun to figure out why First Nations *always* win when land claim treaty obligations and Métis property matters finally go to court, even though cases often take generations to prosecute.

Canada has found ways to accommodate the legitimate concerns of French Québec as a "nation" within this "country." Canada now has an opportunity to seize the sesquicentennial moment to begin redress of the relationship with First Nations, beginning with settlement of longstanding treaty obligations and the facilitation of self-government including control of resources. These are the main prospects for advancement in these long-suffering communities.

The model for control of resources was the successful 1970s resistance of Alberta under Premier Peter Lougheed to a "National Energy Policy" which might have denuded that province of its wealth. This example was emulated by Newfoundland under Premier Danny Williams as oil from that province came on-stream at the turn of the century. Lougheed's mother was Métis so he knew how these things are supposed to work and he defended Alberta accordingly. Williams quarreled with Labrador's Métis population, using their arguments against Ottawa but not in their favour on other issues. If we appear to belabour these matters, it is only to highlight the Canadian model which must now be applied to First Nations on a national scale for the benefit of all.

Steps toward equal partnership in a re-energized Canada will be mapped out in the next chapter, but maximizing the opportunities delineated in the *Report of the Truth and Reconciliation Commission* could be a first step in an historic process in areas such as education and health care. Other Canadians, worried that their hard-earned money paid in taxes is being thrown in vain at First Nations problems, could learn that whatever money is currently expended in Native areas is not from anybody's income tax but from a share of resource development royalties, the tip of the old unfulfilled treaties iceberg.

New Zealand, Bolivia and Denmark have found ways to successfully promote fuller participation of their Aboriginal communities while Australia and most of the Americas lag behind in a manner not unlike Canada's. In the USA it is "states rights" advocates who have insured that the "lower mainland" remains as backward as any part of the world in relation to Aboriginal development, while in Hawaii and Alaska it is federal leadership which is providing opportunities for Aboriginal advancement through self-government and mutual respect in recent years and going forward with energy and success.

The new provinces of Alberta and Saskatchewan, as well as Newfoundland and Labrador, helped bring Canada into a new era in the twentieth century. Yukon, Denendeh (an alternate folk name for the "Northwest Territories") and Nunavut could do the same for Canada in the twenty-first century. These areas of First Nations majorities or population pluralities could become the engines for sustainable developments in accord with evolving Canadian priorities under their leadership.

Few people in 1905 shared Laurier's optimism that the West could amount to much, but look at the West today! And after years of "Newfie jokes" about being undeveloped and backward, the joke is on other Canadians now, since recently Newfoundlanders have frequently had the highest standard of living (on a ratio of high incomes and low costs), having learned how to manage the Canadian system. Frontier energy and resources can provide a new vision for Canada again in the twenty first century, and, at the same time, redress wrongs which have held back First Nations for so long.

First Nations citizens are ready to take the lead themselves, as illustrated by the determination demonstrated in the *Idle No More* movement, but all Canadians need to partner in this new future for our country. We constructed the Canadian Pacific Railroad from east to west, built the St. Lawrence Seaway from the Atlantic Ocean to the centre of the continent and facilitated the Alaska Highway from Dawson Creek, BC to Fairbanks, Alaska. We did many such things to bring the West along, to serve eastern industry and to provide security for our American neighbours. We need to consider equally colossal undertakings to open up the North and serve its people. Maps which depict the North as gargantuan unpopulated wastelands are untruthful images we hope to overcome in this sesquicentennial season of celebration, introspection and aspiration.

Yukon's First Nations are descended from the earliest settlements in the Americas, having crossed the prehistoric land bridge between Siberia and Alaska some 23,000 years ago. The first "whitecomers" were Russians and the Yukon Museum displays tools and shackles found in defunct gold mines worked by convict labour under the czars. The Klondike gold rush in the 1890s brought a population boom of 100,000 fortune seekers, and various mining enterprises to this day are the only industries surpassing government services in employment. Highways now connect Yukoners east to west and south to north.

Yukon attained local self- government in 1895 when it became a district of the Northwest Territories. Yukon has aspired to provincial status ever since. This goal is unlikely to be achieved until members of

World's Most Northerly Mosque in Inuvik, NWT

the First Nations communities succeed in becoming secure in social and economic engagement. They appear to be ready, willing and able.

The Alaska Highway was built with Canadian assistance during World War II by the American Army Corps of Engineers (1700 miles in 170 days) to meet the threat of Japanese invasion in the panic following Pearl Harbor. This recently paved highway should become more than a means to pass through the Yukon *en route* to a bustling Alaska.

With mosques and temples springing up all across the north, Asian, Middle Eastern and African immigrants are now increasingly supplementing Yukon's white and First Nations populations serving in medical, legal, educational and government services.

Many of these professionals now commit to long term residency and our goal could be a rich cultural mix, with affirmative action programs for First Nations to counterbalance earlier exploitation, as Yukon does become a province, almost certainly within the next fifty years.

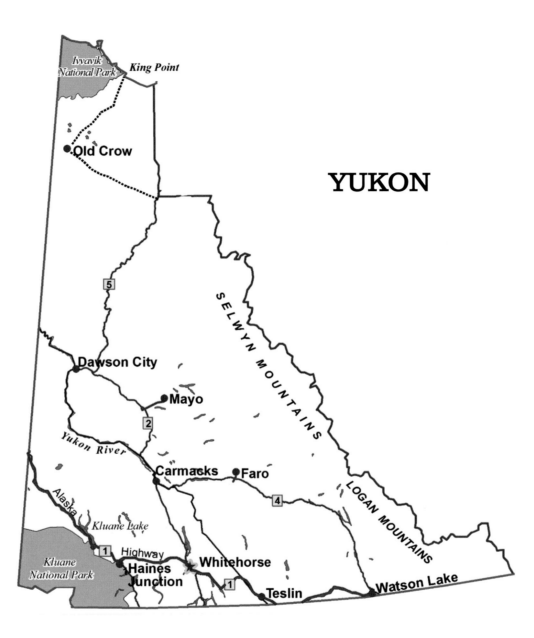

YUKON

Ivvavik National Park — King Point

●Old Crow

SELWYN MOUNTAINS

Dawson City

●Mayo

Yukon River

Carmacks ●Faro

LOGAN MOUNTAINS

Alaska

Kluane Lake

Kluane National Park

Highway

Haines Junction Whitehorse

Teslin Watson Lake

Map P: Yukon Looks Big in the Northern Distortion to Which we are Accustomed, but it is Smaller Than all Provinces Except Some in Atlantic Canada

In the Northwest Territories (or Denendeh) First Nations make up just over half the population, compared with Yukon where they represent less than one third of the total, and Nunavut where more than ninety percent of the population is Inuit. Gold in Yellowknife, diamond mines at the eastern tip of Great Slave Lake, oil in Norman Wells and natural gas off the Arctic coast accounted for growing economic activity in the NWT through the 20th century.

Climate change opens other opportunities as well as challenges to the natural habitat. Canada's Northwest Territories contain two of the ten largest lakes in the world, and unlike the Great Lakes, both are entirely in Canada and neither in areas where human habitation or wildlife is at risk. Each is approximately 10,000 square miles or 30,000 square kilometres in area, together larger than the entire province of Nova Scotia.

A feature of Great Bear Lake and Great Slave Lake which even fewer Canadians might realize is that they are the deepest bodies of water anywhere in the western hemisphere, hundreds of metres deeper than Lake Superior, for example, a lake that supports human habitation in the millions, as well as both industry and wildlife in environmental sustainability. What this stupendous resource could do for themselves and others under First Nations control and management has never been explored.

The outright splendour as well as the opportunities of the north are part of the Canada many of us hardly know, but these sesquicentennial celebrations may give us a new vision as we get to know our country better.

There seems to be no limit to the possibilities in Canada's North, but a needed next step is the creation of a university with satellite campuses in centres like Dawson City in Yukon, Fort Simpson in the NWT, and Kangirlinig (formerly Rankin Inlet) in Nunavut. The splendid Canadian High Arctic Research Station (CHARS), opening in 2018 at Cambridge Bay, should be its first "graduate school."

Then, as the Northwest Passage opens up to regular shipping, there will need to be three deep water ports across the north. These will probably be built at King Point in Yukon, Kugluktuk (Coppermine) in NWT and at South Polaris, adjoining Iqaluit, the capital of Nunavut, the latter under construction already.

All three deep water ports are needed to service ships, to export and import goods, to bring down prices of consumer goods, and to welcome tourists following Frobisher's route. They would also play a peacekeeping military role as we "stand on guard for thee, O Canada," in an era when Russia, the USA and others are testing Canada's claim to sovereignty in the North.

Map Q: With a Mainland Actually Smaller than Ontario, the Northwest Territories Has the Deepest Lakes in the Western Hemisphere

In 1968 a young Jean Chrétien visited the town of St. Paul in Northern Alberta, then still known as St-Paul-des-Métis. The current writer was engaged to introduce the rookie Revenue Minister to the noon hour crowd in the cafeteria at the Co-op, and to conduct him on a tour of the riding. He delivered an impromptu election speech from a stage consisting of four wooden Coke beverage boxes, and then asked to be taken to the nearby Blue Quills Indian Residential School.

At the beginning of the 20th century, attendance at school had been made mandatory for all Aboriginal children between the ages of seven and fifteen. Most tiny remote Aboriginal communities had no schools, but another reason for the bringing of First Nations children to residential schools was the belief that isolation from Indigenous culture was necessary to prepare them for life in Canadian society.

Blue Quills was one of the first such schools, operating under the British first at Lac La Biche since 1862, before confederation, and moved to St. Paul in 1931 where it operated from kindergarten to grade eight. Classes were taught by the Oblate Fathers of Mary Immaculate and by the Grey Nuns of Montréal.

Chrétien was impressed by the dedication of the priests and nuns, and seemed influenced to believe that, except for some unacceptable situations, "abuse" was limited to the use of the strap for discipline, which he had personally experienced as a child in Québec, as had I in Nova Scotia. But Chrétien was also convinced that the Residential Schools were simply inappropriate systemically. He suspected that the more egregious abuse rumoured to take place in such schools might be due primarily to the greater vulnerability of students in that system, and that the schools should be replaced with an education system under Indian control.

Following the election, he took appropriate action as the new Minister of Indian Affairs, but when officials attempted to close Blue Quills in 1971, the Department of Indian Affairs encountered protests from the local First Nations people. Control of the school was turned over to the Blue Quills Native Education Council, who could have been in charge for the previous hundred years, and Blue Quills became the first Canadian residential school administered by Aboriginal people with priests and nuns reporting to them. Blue Quills is now a First Nations college that operates on the principles of Nehiyaw Mamtonecihkan (Indian cultural understanding) and Moniyaw Mamtonecihkan (white academic understanding) in which the second operates within the context of the first.

While he was with me, Chrétien also met students and teachers from the "Protestant" (public) school at Goodfish Lake, where I preached in the church every second Sunday in support of my senior indigenous colleague, the Rev. John Snow. The principal and second teacher were a couple from Leamington, Ontario who early in their career accepted the challenge of their local church minister to serve at Goodfish, where they remained for 20 years. I knew them to be beloved by parents in the church and by students who were being prepared for high school and university, several of whom I still see in the news serving in various professions.

Jean also took a walk to have a private chat with Colin Shirt, the chief elder of our congregation, and then with Sam Bull, the president of our Youth Group, a teenager who lit a fire in the wood burner on Sunday mornings before I got there. I recall Chrétien's words, "what fine people they all are" even as he was schooling me about the systemic injustice inherent in the whole "colonial" structure, as he saw it. Even the best intentioned teachers were in a system which was doomed to fail; a few bad actors in this situation would make it horrendous.

Chrétien recognized that while there may be both good and bad people involved, the basis of the problem was a bad system. While bad people are hard to avoid in any society, they are worse in a bad system. Bad people may not often be reformed but bad systems can be fixed.

In a later ministry at South Peace United Church in Dawson Creek, BC, my organist was a public health nurse who had spent several years in Igaluit. My saddest day with her was when she learned of an RCMP officer charged with physical abuse in her former community.

Her anger at him was palpable as the widow of an RCMP officer she believed had served in the north with honor.

In a subsequent ministry in Moose Jaw, Saskatchewan, one of my leading elders was a recently retired teacher from the residential school at Port Alberni, BC. Far from participating in the reported prohibitions of the use of native languages, this teacher had become fluent in several of them in order to communicate to both students and their parents about the importance of education for their futures. But when media reported the particularly appalling sexual exploitation by one particular teacher at that school, my friend became so ill that we thought he might die.

He was guilty of participation in an historic and systemic evil, despite forty years of dedicated service since his graduation from the University of Toronto in 1950 when the world was so different and needed to be turned upside-down. We are doing that today with Indigenous nurses, Indigenous RCMP officers and Indigenous teachers working along side white colleagues and visible-minority new

Canadian professionals … in both Native and non-Native settings.

Good nurses, police and teachers were acknowledged by many in presentations to the Truth and Reconciliation Commission. Disparaging but true stories of abuse and exploitation made better evening news than analysis of the systemic problems which made the children of First Nations especially vulnerable. In recent years it has been "politically incorrect" to acknowledge the dedicated service of fine professional Canadians in a wrong-headed system, so those in my acquaintance have cowered in silent embarrassment and sorrow. None of this is to deny or diminish the horrors of the residential school system, but to also testify to a continuing reservoir of good will.

Some sense that good relationships may have predominated over bad is supported by census statistics indicating that a clear majority of First Nations citizens continue to identify with Roman Catholic, Anglican and United Church religious traditions, which themselves have now been enriched by the "older testaments" of Native spirituality.

The Anglican Cathedral of St. Jude, Often Called "the Igloo Cathedral," Provides Leadership to the Largest Anglican Diocese in the World

The "Igloo Cathedral" in Iqaluit, originally built by local volunteers, was burned by an arsonist in 2005. It has been rebuilt at a cost of ten million dollars through a building fund over 12 years, with a goal of being finished in the sesquicentennial year with a thousand First Nations members and friends pledging $20.00 a week in extra offerings.

This Anglican cathedral is certainly "self-governing" as the seat of the Diocese of the Arctic, which covers the Northwest Territories, Nunavut, and Nunavik region of Northern Québec. With ninety percent Indigenous membership and clergy, and daily worship in both Inuktitut and English, it administers the greatest area of any Anglican diocese in the world.

This cathedral is well known for its splendid liturgical artwork, the product of Inuit craftsmanship, including such items as wall hangings, woven collection baskets, a cross made many years ago of narwhal tusks and a carved soapstone baptismal font roooucd from the old cathedral. That font had been dedicated by Queen Elizabeth II, always popular

It Would be Hard not to Worship
in the Stunning Northern Setting
of Whitehorse United Church

among First Nations, during a visit to Iqaluit in 2002, when she flawlessly employed the Inuit liturgy, "Nakurmiit ammalu quviasuigitsi" in her words of blessing.

Indeed, the complexities of the North are reflected in religious life across the three Territories, deserving some attention. If 90% of the worshippers at St. Jude's are Inuit, attendance at the beautiful United Church in Whitehorse is approximately 90% Caucasian, with a smattering of First Nations members and a few non-white New Canadians.

Meanwhile, participation in activities at the United Church in Yellowknife,

including its towering community service facility, appears to be 40% Caucasion, 50% First Nations and 10% non-white New Canadian.

At the same time, there remains bedrock Roman Catholic and Anglican membership in smaller communities, almost entirely Indigenous, along with a Pentecostal phenomenon across the spectrum.

Yellowknife United Church
and its Community Service Tower

Smudging, drumming, animistic amulets and, below the tree line, sweat lodge ceremonies are important communal spiritual expressions, even among the church going First Nations population.

There are a few communities worshipping in explicitly Aboriginal traditions, but this is limited since Catholic, Anglican and United congregations have integrated the "Indigenous old testaments" into their practice. (This is true in indigenous congregations north and south, and increasingly so also in Caucasian majority congregations across Canada.) In the north, Pentecostals maintain the classical European theological base and New Canadians extend the religious landscape in several newly built Islamic mosques and one-room Hindu temples and Buddhist shrines in many mid-sized communities and in larger urban centres.

Religious observance is at a high level in the Canadian north, in concert with religious trends in developing cultures and emerging powers like China, India, Eastern Europe, parts of Africa and much of South America. This is in counter-distinction to the benign secularism in southern Canada and the argumentative atheism of mostly elderly white males of the Eastern Seaboard of the USA and in Western Europe – trends at odds with the growth of religion throughout in the developing world, including Canada's north.

As we find also in the Maritimes, Québec, and other regions, the Canadian North has its own culture, resonating religiously with trends in other political and cultural environments in the world. In this regard Canada's north is increasingly like China, India and rapidly developing parts of Africa, in contrast to spiritually moribund cultures in much of North America and Europe where many people do not know what they believe, and the social order sometimes seems to be disintegrating.

Mention has been made of the need for three deep water ports in the north. King Point in the west is a natural harbour which may be developed to serve traffic as it increases in the future.

In response to immediate needs for supply, industry and tourism in the east, work on the $84,000,000. South Polaris harbour construction began in 2016 for completion in 2020.

Half way through the Northwest Passage, Grays Bay illustrates the way out of the catch-22 whereby the North cannot pay for infrastructure without revenue from development, and cannot obtain revenue from development until the infrastructure is in place. But this project is ready to begin due to cooperation between the Inuit-owned Nunavut Resources Corp., the Kitikmeot Inuit Association, the mining industry, two Territorial governments and the Government of Canada.

This particular development, which will also serve both Cambridge Bay and Kugluktuk ("Coppermine") has been promoted by Senator Denis Patterson of Nunavut. It has recently been fast-tracked by a Transport Canada review headed by former cabinet minister David Emerson, and tabled in the House of Commons on February 26, 2016 by Transport Minister Marc Garneau with a recommendation for "immediate" support.

This infrastructure development would enable the Izok Corridor zinc-lead mining project of Chinese-owned MMG Resources Inc. to proceed with mines proposed for High Lake, 50 kilometres south and Izok Lake, 350 miles south. This is all within the extreme west portion of Nunavut, but the road gets close to Yellowknife near the NWT border, making construction of a long-dreamed-of all-weather road possible from the NWT capital to the Arctic coast, accounting for the support of NWT Premier Bob McLeod for this project.

In presenting the report in the Senate, Senator Patterson summed up as follows, if I may quote from Hansard: "This nation-building project is close to shovel-ready and would require an initial commitment of $34 million from Canada over the next four years to complete the permits and engineering process. Best of all, the Inuit-owned Nunavut Resources Corp. would build and own the road and port, which could also serve the Royal Canadian Navy as a refueling location, and safe landing area for storage and resupply in the region, while collecting long-term lease payments from the mining company in addition to royalties and taxes."

Final infrastructure costs for the port and road have been estimated at $6.5 billion, of which the governments would pay one third, leading then to an estimated $39.49 billion in resource development investments by investors in the mines and concomitant tax revenue to benefit Nunavut. The public share in such developments is small in comparison with railway construction in the west and seaway construction in the east, both of which have brought immeasurable benefits to those regions and to Canada. Nunavut is dotted with mines both working and workable, but this example shows the importance of infrastructure.

Nunavut is also Canada's interface with Russia's future mid-Arctic borders. Our North is defended by a volunteer military force made up of Inuit, First Nations, Métis and some occasional non - Aboriginals.

These 5,000 "Canadian Rangers" serve in various communities across the entire north, uniformed in red sweatshirts and baseball caps issued by the Canadian Military, along with World War II surplus rifles. They are "ready for the Ruskies," in the established Canadian tradition of peacekeeping, should the Russians encroach upon our portion of the Arctic Ocean recognized by international law, or should they approach our shore. This is not exactly a shabby outfit, thanks to their devotion to duty, so we are not denigrating the service provided by the proud Rangers, especially when the cameras roll during the usual Prime Minister's annual tour of the North. However, their rag-tag presence is a perfect symbol of the neglect, the underfunding, the inadequacy and the lack of vision Canada has exhibited in reference to both First Nations as a whole and the North in particular in our first 150 years.

Let's add three permanent military bases to the list of three universities and three ports. Office locations of CFNA HQ Whitehorse and CFNA HQ Yellowknife should expand and go to more strategic locations in Yukon and Northwest Territories, and CFS Alert in Nunavut will get special consideration in the *"Grand Finale"* at the end of this souvenir book.

Map R: Nunavut as a Treasure Trove of Everything the World Needs or Wants – All Now Under First Nations Inuit Control

It's Already Happening in the North

Preface to Chapter Four by Hon. Larry Bagnell, MP for Yukon

With forewords about the past and the present by my parliamentary and other colleagues, Brian Arthur Brown has given us pictures of Canada in the nineteenth and twentieth centuries in a series of glorious images, though he gives them to us "warts and all." It falls to me to introduce Canada in the twenty-first century by illustrating how things predicated by Dr. Brown have already begun to take shape.

I suggested to him the inevitability of three deep water ports on Canada's Arctic coast. These might be, among other potential sites, at King Point, Grays Bay, and South Polaris, the first in the west near Alaska, the second half way through the Northwest Passage, and a third at Iqaluit in the east. The east and west coasts of Canada are lined with federally owned and operated ports, while not one full port yet exists along Canada's longest coastline.

Brown has called for a university in the Territories, and the good news is that Yukon College is approved to become a university by 2021, with several sub-campus locations in Yukon, First Nations Initiatives for students from north and south, and credit transferability from Community Colleges in the other Territories. Students from NWT and Nunavut are already on campus, studying at Whitehorse in degree programs presented by the University of Regina (Bachelors in Education and Social Work) and the University of Alberta (Bachelors in Northern Sciences and in Environmental Conservation). Three of the eight members of the Board of Governors of the college are First Nations governors, a proportion which will continue in the university. Present degree programs will continue, college diploma programs like Visual Arts will be upgraded to university standards, and a respected college program in Public Administration (key to First Nations advancement) will culminate in a degree program as a Bachelor of Business Administration.

This book about Canada at the sesquicentennial juncture has a special emphasis on First Nations in Canada, celebrating some dramatic advances in their status, and acknowledging that until many left so far behind share in those advances, our country cannot hope to achieve its full potential. Full participation is proceeding apace in the Northwest Territories, Nunavut is a model for the nation and the world, as are Yukon First Nations who are increasingly moving to the fore in these matters.

Since historic treaties were never signed in Yukon, the governments of Canada and Yukon are now in the ongoing stages of implementing modern-day treaties for individual First Nations through the land claims process based on an Umbrella Agreement of 2008 and rooted in the Constitutional Act of Canada in 1982. Yukon has 14 First Nations and while some details of implementation remain to be worked out, settlement of land claims to date has provided 11 of them with access, rights, and obligations in reference to land and resources, and the right to govern their own affairs.

First Nations self-government in Yukon is supported by a modern bureaucracy administered by Indigenous professionals. Native involvement in environmental concerns reflects a commitment to both sustainable development and protection of the natural world. Those young people, increasingly engaged in educational, sporting, cultural and high tech pursuits, are rarely featured in news reports of misery and dead-end prospects, leading to suicide among Native youths elsewhere.

But while the First Nations are the largest population group in Yukon, at 25% of the total, the largest single group of non-Indigenous residents is of Philippine origin at 10%, followed by smaller populations of English, French, Scottish, Irish, Chinese, Japanese, and various other European and other groups from around the world. This compares with Indigenous populations of 22% in Labrador, 20% in Saskatchewan, 18% in Manitoba, 52% in NWT, 90% in Nunavut and smaller but significant proportions of the population in every other province. Like the Cree of northern Québec, the Territories in the North are providing models for the full participation of First Nations so desperately needed in northern Ontario and elsewhere. At the same time, as indicated, new Canadian visible minorities play an increasing role here.

While there are health care workers, I do not yet observe many First Nations physicians in Yukon. First Nations lawyers, some trained in Victoria and Ottawa, are fully engaged in the legal profession and the courts. Teachers and teaching assistants in schools in outlying and First Nations communities of Yukon are both Native and non-Native, and that is also the case in the schools and colleges of the capital city.

Provincial status for all three Territories would be possible and appropriate now if the present financial regime could remain in place while the above developments continue to unfold. "Have-not" provinces receive federal transfers in the form of "equalization payments." The Territories receive bulk fiscal transfers in a Formula Funding Agreement which may need to continue for some time. In essence, the majority of the Territorial Government budgets in each territory flow unrestricted to the territorial government from the federal government, which recoups a certain amount of that through taxes, royalties, leases, fees and other sources.

These Territories still require this guarantee, as did Newfoundland for sixty years after joining Confederation, even turning over large debts to Ottawa, which the Territories are not proposing to do. All three Territories have been involved in a process of "devolution" in recent years, whereby almost all powers enjoyed by provinces are being transferred (except for some revenue resources maintained by the federal authority) under the still necessary Formula Funding Agreement.

As the international Vice-Chair of the Standing Committee of Parliamentarians of Arctic Regions, I am aware of some interest in Russia making up for lost time by copying the best examples of twenty first century advances in self-government and resource management by Canadian First Nations, particularly in the north, where Russia has significant Indigenous populations. For that matter, the Dalai Lama has expressed to me interest in our First Nations self-government model as a template for what Tibet should aspire toward within China.

I moved to Whitehorse 35 years ago and would never want to leave. The secretary at my church recently described the lifestyle here as "Canada's best kept secret," having moved here from Ottawa to find a climate that is almost the same (cold but manageable winters and warm blissful summers). The cultural scene is not exceeded by much anywhere, amenities in a place like Whitehorse are unparalleled, and the pace of life is a contrast between the regular rush hour elsewhere and the occasional rush minute here. The clean air and pure water attracted a Washington patent lawyer of my acquaintance to live here and to work online in a high tech environment as efficient as any available in the US Capitol. I am pleased that many Canadians are getting to know our country better, and that the North is increasingly a part of everybody's Canada.

Larry Bagnell

Opportunities in the North with the Maturation of Territories and New Provinces in the Next Hundred Years

Opportunities abound in the North with the maturation of territories and new provinces in the next hundred years. Canada is now a multicultural country. That much is a given, but how did we get to this place? This matter may be worth some detailed consideration in this sesquicentennial exercise.

In the twenty-first century the questions of who would dominate in Canada, English or French, First Nations or Europeans, Protestants or Catholics, have been relegated to history, dissipated finally by the multicultural nature of the country and a commitment to equal rights for all. These developments took form mid twentieth-century, with roots further back.

As recounted by Ian Greene in *The Charter of Rights* (1989, published by James Lorimer and Company), in 1936, four years before being elected to Parliament, John Diefenbaker began drafting his Bill of Rights. As a young boy, he saw injustice first-hand in the form of discrimination against French-Canadians, Natives, Métis and European immigrants. In 1950, a decade before the Canadian Bill of Rights became law, Diefenbaker, then a Saskatchewan MP, was already giving speeches about why such a law was needed. "Individuals' freedoms of religion, press, speech and association are threatened by the state," he said. "A Bill of Rights is needed to take a forthright stand against discrimination based on colour, creed or racial origin."

In 1960, as prime minister, Diefenbaker successfully legislated the Canadian Bill of Rights, the precursor of the Canadian Charter of Rights and Freedoms in the constitutional reforms of 1982, promulgated by Pierre Elliott Trudeau. The latter formulation built on the former, but also upon a succession of such charters dating back to *The Declaration of the Rights of Man and of the Citizen (Déclaration des droits de l'homme et du citoyen)*, passed by the National Constituent Assembly of France in August 1789, as a fundamental document of the French Revolution. It was introduced by General Lafayette who had been working with US President Thomas Jefferson in preparing the US Bill of Rights, and enshrined in the first ten amendments to the Constitution of the United States. In Canada this legal tradition is treasured in the Napoleonic Code which is the basis of civil law in Québec and which passed its egalitarian ideals to the rest of the country in the current Constitution.

By this time Diefenbaker had already used his Bill of Rights mandate to name James Gladstone of Alberta as the first Native senator and Ellen Fairclough of Ontario as the first female cabinet minister in Canada.

In 1962, as Immigration Minister, Fairclough introduced new regulations intended to eliminate racial discrimination in immigration policy. She also implemented a more generous policy on refugees, and dramatically increased the number of immigrants allowed into Canada, mainly through extending processing offices beyond the United Kingdom and Europe to all parts of the British Commonwealth in particular.

Ellen Fairclough is the unacknowledged mother of multi-cultural Canada. It was these developments which broadened the character of the country as we know it today, though implementation of her vision depended on her Conservative successor Richard Bell and then a succession of Liberal ministers under Prime Minister Lester B. Pearson. Indeed, this combining of a progressive immigration policy with commitment to the rights of all became a hallmark of the political leadership of Pierre Elliott Trudeau, Brian Mulroney and Jean Chrétien in alternation between Conservative and Liberal regimes through the balance of the twentieth century.

Canada broadened and deepened itself as New Canadians enriched the country in large numbers in an atmosphere of acceptance which has avoided the divisions over immigration and refugees characterizing both Europe and America in the twenty-first century.

This national evolutionary trend became noticeable in urban centres across Canada in the late twentieth century, dramatically affected the north beginning around the turn of the twenty-first century, and is slowly becoming more evident in small towns and rural Canada in the current sesquicentennial era.

The impact of "New Canadian" influence in the North is of particular interest at this point in our story. Many New Canadians are especially well qualified in the professions and have settled in the North where their skills have been needed and certification is more easily recognized under federal jurisdiction. The presence of these engineers, doctors, teachers and government workers has a special role to play in preparing the territories of the region for provincial status.

As an interesting aside, the most obvious illustration of the trend is strong anecdotal evidence offered by residents suggesting that a plurality of health care workers, attending physicians and specialists at the Whitehorse Hospital, and perhaps a majority of doctors in Yellowknife and Iqaluit are visible minority New Canadians, with such personnel also evident in small northern communities.

Following our achievement in successfully integrating immigrants, the next step in Canada's full development is to extend those two policy factors (human rights and the incorporation of large heterogeneous populations) to First Nations as dynamically as we have done in the last half century with New Canadians.

For their part First Nations might facilitate this cultural and economic shift by employing "identity politics" for a transitional period. There may be forty federal constituencies where First Nations voters have a plurality of at least one third, enough to elect a "Treaty Party" (or some similar name), not to form a government but a balance of power position, ready to cooperate with a government prepared to settle their legal claims.

With fast-growing populations already larger than some original provinces in the 19th century, Yukon, Denendeh and Nunavut may very soon have reasonable claims to status as provinces. They may need initial "equalization payments," like some provinces, and infrastructure like the railroad originally built to facilitate British Columbia, but they will be net contributors in the near future.

For example, while Canada has never before contemplated selling fresh water to the United States, the perils associated with climate change there may leave our neighbour in crisis in the next decade or so, with drought and forest fires in a truly calamitous situation even beyond that which we have begun to see now.

The Great Bear and Great Slave Lakes in the NWT are among the ten largest lakes in the world. They are also the two deepest lakes in the western hemisphere, but neither of them is supporting much flora or fauna, nor any very significant human habitation.

Until now, selling water has been a taboo subject in our national discourse, but here we are considering water that is just draining into the Arctic Ocean, which hardly needs more water, with its melting ice caps and rapidly rising sea levels. This makes it possible for the first time to consider diverting water to rescue both rural food producers and city dwellers in places like California, should climate change bring about crises of catastrophic proportions.

Contemplation of this long unthinkable subject could only happen with agreed First Nations control and management built on environmentally sound provisions protecting both our own wildlife habitat and all conceivable future human needs. Water may be more valuable than oil in the future and, in this case, nobody need worry about spills or leaks harming anything *en route*.

First Nations' vigilance on such matters has earned them the confidence of the nation regarding protection of the environment, and First Nations alone hold legal status in respect to management, since both lakes are within long-agreed treaty boundaries, not yet fully implemented.

Moreover, though most other Canadians are unaware of it, First Nations members can freely cross the border for the purposes of immigration, work, education and trade. This is a treaty right recognized by both governments following the meetings between Joseph Brant and George Washington. Article III of the 1794 Jay Treaty between Canada and the USA declared the right of "Indians born in Canada" to trade and travel between the United States and Canada. This right was restated as recently as 1952 in section 289 of the U.S. Immigration and Naturalization Act.

Both the safeguards and the billions of dollars in annual benefits should obviously be under First Nations control. Could payment come partly in the form of cheap fresh produce flown in year round? Canadian naysayers and doom forecasters in media, academia and environmental societies might have very little to say about all this since Canadian First Nations have a natural affinity with the USA including American Natives in danger from drought and fire in a situation worsening annually. The whole relationship between First Nations and the USA goes well beyond affection, and possibly supersedes the fears and the concerns of other Canadians.

In such a situation, northern First Nations would negotiate with the USA and with southern First Nations in Canada to achieve delivery approvals. In this regard even pipelines are not passé. The route from Great Bear Lake to Great Slave Lake would connect with a chain of lakes through Saskatchewan to Lake Winnipegosis. This could be achieved by reversing the flow of the Slave River to Lesser Slave Lake at the edge of the northern watershed, onward south through natural waterways, sluice canals and pipelines, and thence to California.

To the recent surprise of some Canadians, both Indigenous and non-Indigenous, there are First Nations bands that support the oil industry and its pipelines. A similar situation regarding water would be even less counter-intuitive. This book supports neither, but does support a greater measure of control being transferred to First Nations who may be trusted to faithfully represent the national interest (and international) as well as their own concerns.

If a 2000-mile oil pipeline from Alberta to Texas could be built by others, a 1,000-mile Native water pipeline from Manitoba to California would be a cinch, should this previously unthinkable situation come to pass in a catastrophic crisis.

These lakes drain into the Mackenzie River which pours fresh water into the Arctic Ocean at the rate of 10,000 cubic metres per second (or nearly one and a half trillion bathtubs per day).

Preliminary estimates suggest that diversion of twenty percent of that water would be all America could ever need. This level of diversion would not be missed in the ocean any more than anybody now notices the diversion of that much water every day for hydroelectric purposes in Ontario, water which used to flow over the Niagara Falls.

None of the engineering involved in this proposal comes even close to the challenges of building Canada's original railroad, the Alaska Highway or the St. Lawrence Seaway, all for the benefit of non-Aboriginals. Climate change, which threatens to ruin California, could establish the NWT as the saviour of America with immense benefits to the First Nations stewards of this precious resource. This is but one example of a clean and bountiful North, and of possible benefits, once First Nations assume responsibility in their domains.

First Nations' assumption of the control and management of life-giving water over half the continent is in their hands, but this example illustrates the enormous scale of their responsibility and influence once the treaties are fully implemented and self-government is fully realized. There are other examples in the North and elsewhere, and there is no doubt that First Nations leaders and people are ready for these responsibilities. They will decide between issues like traditional Canadian resistance to water export, the needs of a neighbour, the risks of rising sea levels in the Arctic and the benefits to First Nations in food, employment and financial resources.

Meanwhile, there may also be a need for such future territorial political mechanisms for sustainable resource development to cover education, health and other services for First Nations residents of Northern Ontario, Nord-du-Québec and Labrador on a basis equal to other Canadians. Demeaning and ever-increasing grants from the federal government will never come close to the actual benefits owed to First Nations through simple fulfillment of treaty provisions long languishing in the courts.

Northern Ontario and Labrador already have political parties seeking provincial status and the First Nations of Québec are now getting organized in regard to becoming a territory. Like current territories, far north portions of Ontario, Québec and Newfoundland have population increases at rates above the national average. They have First Nation majorities, and resources from treaty and land claims settlements to provide the capital for wise and sustainable development. The required capital will be no more difficult to raise than in the cases of building the Canadian Pacific Railway, the Alaska Highway or the St. Lawrence Seaway … infinitesimal increases to the national debt with benefits for all Canada.

Might some of these entities become provinces in order to attain decision making power over their affairs? What follows may seem like just a floating of ideas, pipe dreams or fantastic illusions, until we consider the improbable stories of provinces coming into being in previous eras, the history of boundary changes during the past one hundred and fifty years, and the appropriate desires of those in remote regions for self-government equal to that enjoyed by other Canadians. This may apply especially to First Nation Indians, Inuit and Métis peoples in particular.

With a rising population of 50,000, Labrador is approaching the threshold for provincial status and will arrive there sometime within the next fifty years, about the same time as Yukon.

The Labrador Party is seeking provincial status and as far back as 1971 its leader, Tom Burgess, was elected to the Newfoundland and Labrador Legislative Assembly with 50.3% of the vote. Ern Condon succeeded him as leader in 2003, followed by Ron Barron in 2007. When the party runs in the four Labrador ridings it usually polls between one tenth and one third of the electorate so far. The Labrador Party has not run candidates in recent elections, preferring to work with First Nations organizations in the courts, and educating people in preparation for the propitious moment, which may be approaching sooner than many Canadians might expect.

In 2002 a Royal Commission concluded that public pressure by Labradoreans seeking provincial status needs to be taken seriously, as claimed by the Assembly of First Nations on behalf of Labrador's Innu Nation in 1999. Northern Labrador, known as Nunatsiavut, recently attained municipal self-government, and the southern area of Nunatukavut expects the same upon settlement of a major land claim.

Labrador has an international airport and armed forces facilities in Goose Bay and Happy Valley. It has hydroelectric dams and iron ore mines in Labrador City and Wabush, fishing communities on the coast and plans for eventual mining activity at the world's largest nickel deposits in Voisey's Bay.

The Labrador West campus of Newfoundland's College of the North Atlantic in Labrador City has 200 full time students and Contract Training and Continuing Education courses for 500 participants per year. It also serves Wabush and Churchill Falls with potential for significant expansion. Health care and other amenities are also available but embryonic.

Roads are needed down the St. Lawrence to Québec and up the Atlantic coast to outlying communities. A Labrador legislative building at Cartwright and a resident civil service would then cure many complaints by people seeking provincial status for what was previously called "A Dependency of Newfoundland."

North Aulatsivik Island

Saglek Bay

LABRADOR SEA
MER DU LABRADOR

South Aulatsivik Island

Nain
Voisey's Bay

Hopedale

Makkovik
Postville
Cape Harrison

LABRADOR

Michikaman Lake

Rigolet

Cartwright

Churchill Falls
North West River

labrador City
Wabush

Happy Valley-Goose Bay

Port Hope
Simpson

QUEBEC

L'Anse au Loup
Forteau

Map S: Labrador, a Dependency of Newfoundland or a Province of Canada?

In Northern Québec's Nunavik area the Northern Cree have already availed themselves of political experience related to Québec Hydro. They have joined their Inuit neighbors in moving toward territorial status as a bilingual Inuit-French society, the basis of a future Nunavik province.

If indeed all science points to Hudson Bay becoming "The Baltic Sea of North America" over the next hundred years, just the next twenty-five years should be transformative, with the governments of both Canada and Québec facilitating territorial status for Nunavik, as a prelude to eventual provincehood. The coming societal and economic activity will require infrastructure which should be put into place now; not just seaports and airports, but also educational and health facilities.

Imagine Indigenous provincial parliament buildings at Kuujjuaq, the present administrative centre on the southern shore of Ungava Bay. To play a role similar to what has grown to be Memorial University in Canada's youngest province of Newfoundland, consider a French and First Nations community college at stunning Inukjuak,

where *Nanook of the North* was filmed in 1922 as North America's first full length documentary.

Picture a deep water port near the golden sand dunes of the twin communities of Kuujjuarapik and Whapmagoostui where the Grand River empties into Hudson Bay. There a decent airport and an old US / Canadian joint military base await upgrades to serve our country's needs. Among fifteen other major population centres where the residents are over 95% Inuit, the largest are Puvirnituk and Salluit.

Québec is now more secure about the French reality in Canada, and its middle north is also maturing to the stage in which its own interests would be best served as a new unilingual French province we might call Québec Nordique. If the majority in the Northern area of Nunavik is Inuit, a plurality in the Nordique middle are Cree First Nations.

In April of 1971 the Québec government announced plans for a massive hydroelectric project in the James Bay region, intending to serve the needs of the province and export power to the United States.

On November 15, 1973 The Québec Association of Indians won an injunction blocking the construction of the project on their traditional territory, pending settlement of a long delayed land claim or adequate participation in the project on their part. In 1974 The court's "Malouf Judgement" confirmed Québec's legal obligation to negotiate a treaty covering the territory, even as construction proceeded.

The Grand Council of the Crees (*Eeyou Istchee*), representing the Cree communities of Northern Québec, was then created to better protect Cree rights during negotiations with the governments of Quebec and Canada. The leader of this organization, and National Chief of the First Nations of Canada (2000-2003), Matthew Coon Come is highly respected and continues to this day in providing models of First Nations cultural security, productivity, prosperity and Indigenous peoples' participation in the life of the world of the twenty-first century. His story, to which we shall return, points to the enduring ability of First Nations to produce brilliant leaders whose political abilities have rarely been appreciated or applied to national issues.

Map T: Québec as Three Provinces a Hundred Years from Now 2117?

On November 11, 1975 the governments of Canada and Québec and representatives from each of the Cree villages and affected Inuit villages signed the James Bay and Northern Quebec Agreement. It offered a modern "nation to nations" treaty styled contract explicitly describing the rights and opportunities of the Indigenous people. This hydroelectric treaty became a model for future conflicts in other communities with issues of the same nature. It allowed hydroelectric development on Cree lands in exchange for financial compensation, greater autonomy, and improvements to health care, housing, employment opportunities and educational services. The progressive lifestyle in the communities of Québec Cree today has become an inspiration to Indigenous communities all around the world.

Matthew Coon Come was born in 1956 on his parents trapline at Mistissini, Quebec. He excelled academically at the La Tuque Indian Residential School before studying political science, economics, and law at Trent and McGill Universities. He also undertook theological studies in the United States following his tenure as

Grand Chief Matthew Coon Come

National Chief of the Assembly of First Nations, serving briefly as a Pentecostal pastor in an Ottawa congregation upon his return.

His facing down of the government of Quebec and Hydro Quebec was achieved by applying Canadian law to an opportunity for systemic solutions to the First Nations conundrum, rather than appeals to moral justice or complaining about prejudice.

When the rights of all of the Indigenous peoples in Québec were put at risk by the 1995 Québec Referendum, Mathew Coon Come achieved national notoriety by asserting the Crees' or Eeyou Istchee right of self-determination through their own referendum. He insisted on the right of Québec's First Nations to remain in Canada with their territory intact, should Québec ever succeed.

Matthew was informed by this author that at least one "progressive" member of the Conservative Party of Canada is of the opinion that the best way they could hope win a future election would be to elect him as their leader in their 2017 leadership convention. He chortled, "I am not a member but I guess I could be seen as the perfect candidate for them economically, spiritually and even politically. I also have equally good relations with the Liberals, the NDP and the Green parties but this is not going to happen, at least not just yet." At some point soon there could be a major breakthrough of First Nations in Canadian politics. It may be premature to think of a First Nations Prime Minister, but Mr. Trudeau, what about Matthew Coon Come for Governor General?

While many of the Québec Cree speak Native Languages, and some continue to maintain English as a second language, Section 16 of the treaty agreement specifies that "The Cree School Board will pursue as an objective the use of French as a language of instruction so that pupils graduating from its school will, in the future, be capable of continuing their studies in a French school, college or university elsewhere in Québec, if they so desire." This provision has had the effect, forty years later, of enabling the Québec Cree First Nations to now participate fully in the French culture of Québec.

The Québec which fostered and entered Confederation 150 years ago contained neither Nunavik nor the Nordique, but doubled in size in the nineteenth century to gain the latter, and then doubled again in the twentieth century to gain the former.

In what we are calling Québec Nordique, the *Université du Québec en Abitibi-Témiscamingue* is already established with campuses in both Val-d'Or and Rouyn-Noranda. Picture new provincial parliament buildings like those in Newfoundland at Chibougamau, site of a now-closed military base. Mining, forestry and hydro activities will support health, educational and infrastructure.

This is not a malicious proposal to divide and someday take back the territories ceded to Québec by the crown following confederation in both the nineteenth and twentieth centuries. Such a plot was a non-starter even during the twentieth century campaigns for Québec independence. This proposal is presented in the confidence that Québec will now never leave Confederation.

In an historic forty-year process, 1976-2016, Quebec attained all it needs to fulfill its destiny as a nation within Canada. A second unilingual French province in the middle North of Québec is part of a vision which would strengthen the future of the French nation within Canada which may have more than one bilingual province as well.

A secure and mature Québec of the 21st century could enhance the position of French Canada by thus evolving into two new unilingual provinces and a French/Inuit bi-lingual one which functions comfortably in the context of French Canada.

Expectations are realistic that Yukon and Labrador should become provinces within the next twenty-five years, and that Denendeh and Nunavut may achieve that status before our bicentennial, fifty years from now. Are there other provinces-in-waiting in addition to two possibilities in northern Québec?

Our speculations about Québec are merely in accord with good sense and the Canadian pattern of development, though whether or not the unique hopes and fears of French Canada can ever allow that vision to come to natural fruition may still be open to question. Similar prospects of such evolution in Ontario are more likely than most Canadians imagine. Southern Ontarians may find the idea surprising but acceptable.

Politically and economically the northern parts of that province are seen by some southerners as a nuisance and an unfortunate expense. Ontario's far

North, inhabited almost exclusively by First Nations, is regarded as a problem nobody knows how to fix, a genuine concern but also an embarrassment that so-called "third world" conditions are found in Canada. The advantages for the middle-North of Ontario as a province are obvious, but the evolution of another province in part of old Keewatin in the far north may be the most exciting and fruitful development in Canada in the next hundred years.

In the middle North, the Northern Ontario Heritage Party was formed in 1977 to campaign for provincial status for Northern Ontario. No member has yet been elected to the Legislative Assembly of Ontario, but the party was revived in 2010 under its long time leader, Ed Deibel of North Bay, and re-registered by Elections Ontario.

A flare-up of support for provincial status erupted in 2016 in a spinoff led by Trevor Holliday of Callander, near North Bay. This spontaneous movement was coming more into public consciousness as we approached our sesquicentennial year. A Sudbury Star poll in the spring of 2016 revealed 77% felt Northern Ontario would be better off as a province.

Holliday promoted a petition supporting provincial status which got 10,000 signatures before 2017. This petition is supported by Deibel as godfather of the movement.

With pages of signatures in Algoma, Manitoulin, Kapaskasing, Kenora, Nipissing, Timiskaming, Parry Sound, Muskoka, Sault Ste. Marie, Sudbury, Thunder Bay, Rainy River, Timmins and James Bay, as well as North Bay, the petition begins: "Whereas: The Ontario Government has caused a divide of this beautiful province and vacating as well as segregation of the People of the North in order to solely get votes and not worry about the outcome or effects on Northern Ontario, therefore an expansion of provinces is needed."

Roughly worded and needing refinement, it is expected to be presented in the Ontario Legislature by a northern member already elected by another party. This petition may be the tip of an iceberg that somehow floated into Hudson Bay where First Nations even further north in Ontario have a more urgent need for self-government and control of their resources in a territory or province of their own. Such a development further north, considered below, might pave the way for the aspirations of Deibel and Holliday for a mid-corridor province in the middle north, which might otherwise languish for another hundred years.

The middle North of Ontario is certainly resource rich through a vast swath of rural areas and small towns. Thunder Bay, Sault Ste. Marie, North Bay and Sudbury are all major urban centres. Larger than the biggest cities in some provinces, they would be "players" in the fabric of Canadian life were they not overshadowed by Toronto, Ottawa, Hamilton, London and a dozen other such centres in the "golden horseshoe" surrounding Lake Ontario. They languish as backwaters neglected and ignored in a provincial version of the old National Policy – "send us your resources and we'll sell them back to you at value added prices."

Some northerners feel that resource taxation, expenditures, transportation, and the abandonment of First Nations all benefit Southern Ontario. Legislation from a provincial parliament building rising over Lake Superior at, say, Sault Ste. Marie, could change all that.

A million people live in the middle-North of Ontario, represented by a mere 11 members of the provincial legislature – compared with 44 reps for half that population and half the territory in Newfoundland, for example. Northern Ontario Heritage Party candidates will run in all 11 ridings in the 2018 provincial election. If Deibel and Holliday ever add First Nations and French Canadians to their supporters a new province or two is a done deal. All it would take would be a promise of bilingual services and the settlement of land claims.

As concerns Ontario, the utter desolation of First Nations even further north in the James Bay Lowlands is in the news every year. This is the desperate North commended to Prime Minister Trudeau by Gord Downey of the Tragically Hip band at their final concert on August 20, 2016. Evacuations due to flooding, fire, water borne disease and maladies suffered in few other "developed" countries in the world are endemic here. High unemployment, poor living conditions, lack of educational opportunities and a plethora of social problems exist in communities near recently discovered "Ring of Fire" chromium deposits, perhaps the largest mining prospect in the history and future of Canada.

Images of First Nations for many are dilapidated housing, broken water systems, flooding, missing persons and murder. The dignity and self-reliance of First Nations in Northern Quebec, parts of British Columbia and in the Territories based on systemic approaches goes largely unreported. It is an urgent necessity that all social, environmental, political, economic, infrastructural and educational tools be brought to bear in the provision of resource control and First Nations self-government in the resource rich far-north of Ontario, first as a Territory and eventually as a Province.

As far back as 1876 it was realized that this area was too remote to be properly governed from Toronto, Winnipeg or Ottawa, leading to the abortive creation of Keewatin. Following advice of the Indigenous leaders then consulted, the name "Keewatin" was derived from Algonquin root words, either *giiwedin* (ᑭᐧᐁᑎᐣ) in Ojibwe language or *kīwēhtin* (ᑭᐧᐁᐦᑎᐣ) in Cree — both of which mean "north wind."

The bulge at the bottom of our next map included all of Ontario north of our Laurentia. It is this area which might now become a First Nations Territory and eventually a Province. Instead of resources and royalties going south, Keewatin could then process resources in sustainable development and keep the royalties in place of paltry grants which normally come back as a portion of what is taken out.

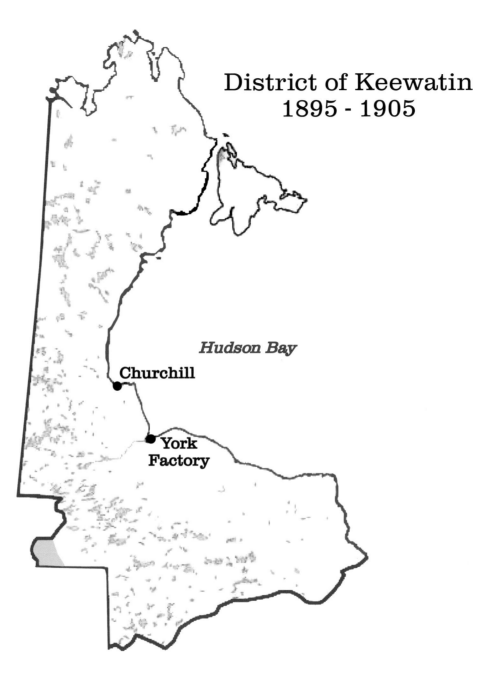

District of Keewatin
1895 - 1905

Hudson Bay

Churchill

York Factory

Map U: The Bulge at the Bottom of Keewatin is the Bulk of a New First Nations Territory or Province to be Carved out of Northern Ontario

In the early years of Canada, there were insufficient resources to finance a separate government for this region, and the First Nations population was much smaller than it is today. Resource discoveries and a quadrupling of the population in recent decades are "game changers" which now justify the initial instincts of both Aboriginals and government officials who sensed a need for self-government in this region.

There is an urgent necessity for the revival of the dream of a Keewatin territory and eventually a province, north of Laurentia, south of Hudson Bay and west of James Bay – all of Ontario north of the fiftieth line of latitude. Perhaps we should even return the east wedge of Manitoba to Keewatin, not shown on our map.

In a world class "Ring of Fire" chromite mining and smelting project, Keewatin has an economic potential said to be equal to the energy resources of Alberta at the height of its economy. Chromite is the ingredient required for stainless steel and Keewatin has fifty percent of the world supply of this highly desirable mineral, as mines in South Africa, India and Kazakhstan become less viable. The development of the Ring of Fire would impact nine Matawa First Nations bands in the immediate vicinity, and 25 other First Nations communities in far-North Ontario.

An unfortunate model is the 2008 opening and closing of the Victor Diamond Mine by De Beers of South Africa, further east near Attawaskapat and Kaseshawan. In the 2009 October international issue of *Mining Magazine* the Victor Mine was proclaimed "Mine of the Year." The diamonds are still there in profuse abundance, but infrastructure and environmental disputes involving First Nations, Ontario and Canada at three levels led De Beers to despair in 2016 and mothball most of the facilities. The solution is the Nunavut model where First Nations self-government works under First Nations control of mineral rights, and land claims are settled before the area becomes a territory *en route* to becoming a province.

Of course, few of these northern riches, which heretofore Ontario has considered its own, will reach world markets through southern routes. Hudson Bay will soon begin to assume its shipping destiny in the heart of Canada, as once envisioned by investors in the company which bears its name. Chartered on May 2, 1670, The Hudson's Bay Company is the oldest incorporated joint-stock merchandising company in the English-speaking world. It will be sad to see the polar bears disappear from the garbage dumps as global warming transforms the city of Churchill at last, but the human social and economic activity in Canada's "Baltic" will be unstoppable. The questions which remain at this sesquicentennial juncture concern the sustainability of the environment as a whole, and the leading role which First Nations have every right to insist upon this time around.

Keewatin may need the same sixty-year guarantee of "equalization" payments that Canada provided to Newfoundland in 1949. Let this be a national priority, lest once again we miss the opportunity to see First Nations fulfill their rightful place in the fabric of Canadian society. With its parliament building overlooking Hudson Bay, its own hospitals, colleges and other amenities, Keewatin has both the resources and the personnel to become a leader rather than a laggard among Canadian territories and provinces.

Map V: Of all Border Changes in the Next Hundred Years, the Re-establishment of Keewatin under First Nations Control is an Urgent Priority

Preface to Chapter Five by the Rt. Rev. David W. Parsons, Bishop of the Arctic

Epiphany in the Snows by Violet Teague

In this picture five Inuit figures include "Joseph," the Madonna and Child, with a shy young Inuit woman bringing her own little baby into this scene in the way that all parents want to expose their children to wonder and the best for their future. The three visitors include a Nascopie Cree hunter from Labrador with a beaver skin, a Hudson's Bay clerk offering fox pelts, and a Métis trader whose walrus tusks are in the hands of Joseph. Dogs replace sheep in this culture where they are more than pets, and reindeer replace camels in a country which has many of the first and none of the second, even in southern pageants where Christmas churchgoers almost forget what country they live in.

Epiphany in the Snows is a scene that most of Canadians can relate to, but it suggests that if the North is to help lead Canada into a meaningful future, Inuit, First Nations, Métis and Europeans are all part of the picture in which Europeans and others will need to adapt themselves to cultures here which go back thousands of years.

This picture might seem merely quaint, but the message for Canada is profound. With values of their own, Inuit, First Nations and Métis will decide for themselves what to select from southern Canadian and world cultures, including European and American values, but they have cultural values of their own to cherish and to apply to modern life. Northern society is changing today as rapidly as the climate, but remains secure and ready to provide needed leadership to Canada in certain respects.

As Brian Brown suggests, First Nations, Inuit and Métis are not merely surviving and struggling to get on their feet. Rather, they are numerous in the millions in Canada now, proud, innovative and strong, and well positioned to help lead our country into the next 50, 100 or 150 years with more than mere material prosperity. Could this be the final delight and best surprise of the sesquicentennial celebrations? For those just getting to know this Canada, we have some wonderful news. There are diamonds, deposits of gold, pure water, gas and oil and many other treasures in the north, but the Native peoples of Canada may be among the richest resources of this land. A final push toward settlement of outstanding treaties with Indigenous Canadians will point the way forward in accessing these resources in a sustainable future.

Without the full participation of Indigenous peoples, and their contributions to the full life of the country, Canada is at risk of what Brian Brown has called the "Mississippi syndrome," a situation in which a non-productive and excluded element of society ultimately drags down the whole. The wisdom of the Inuit people, for example, are their sciences of spirit filled culture. Spirit and culture appear increasingly divorced in the Canadian south and other parts of the "advanced" world, as compared to the developing parts of the world, including the Canadian north. This could be a profound problem for Canada, but the solution is at hand.

What we are describing may be seen politically in the consensus approach of tribal councils and territorial governments. John Ralston Saul and Elizabeth May got it right earlier in this book by pointing to Indigenous models the country could build on. In religion this is seen in a devotion to God in churches which are not without blame in past relations, but which have learned to listen and trust the Indigenous people.

The art in every Indigenous village rivals that in the National Gallery in Ottawa, and is seen in fashion styles from boots to sealskin inlay in clothing. I am suggesting that, being in an eclectic country, Canadians should include Indigenous fashion that reflects an ongoing awareness of the ethos of this country, not simply that of Milan or New York. Even technology can be approached holistically. It is perhaps unknown to many

Canadians that Indigenous elders take to technological advances like teenagers, as appears to be the case through the developing world in places like India and China.

There are Canadian ways of doing politics, worshipping, expressing culture, dressing and doing business in which Indigenous models are appropriate contributions for the future of all Canadians. None of this is to suggest that Indigenous communities are without problems. The economic problems are systemic and can be solved. Pockets of drug and alcohol abuse are as severe as in any southern community and city. I was born and raised in Labrador, and like most northerners who are well traveled I can tell you that we have a very positive and hope-filled attitude. There are problems, but as people who face storms we are seeking ways to address them.

The Truth and Reconciliation Commission was an effective wakeup call to the fact that as Canadians we have not been very respectful to the Inuit and First Nations peoples who welcomed the world to its shores, land and resources. Our Peace Tower in Ottawa proclaims that, "Where there is no vision the people perish." Isn't it time for the Inuit, First Nations and Métis people to be included in the vision, so that we do not perish? When the first North Americans have been encouraged and empowered to share in the leadership of this land through self-government, putting their own ideas, wisdom and values into action, I expect that we will receive another wakeup call wondering what took us so long to recognize these realities.

Indigenous and Arctic peoples have a heritage of surviving and thriving. Northern peoples have blasted through the 20th century excelling in all the conveniences and challenges of modern life, and are preparing to face the 21st century with a determination to take ownership in decision-making that affects their land, people and lifestyle. Northerners appreciate and value the wisdom, knowledge and understanding of their elders. It is about time that the media and intellectual leaders of the south realize that the Inuit and First Nations people have more to share than just where Franklin's sunken ships were to be found.

Arctic peoples are innovative and strong. It is time for the Government of Canada, provinces and multinational companies to truly meet the Inuit, First Nations and Métis people as equal partners. We are in an upsizing mentality, strategizing how we may be a benefit to Canada and the world, leaving it better than it was when we were born.

Working interdependently, we should make it a priority that all children be taught, nurtured and cared for in loving families. Families that practically demonstrate God's love, by the mentoring, equipping and training of children, produce peaceful, compassionate leaders who bless others and help communities prosper. Whether living off the land, or being political leaders to help with self-determination or cultural and economic stewardship, we want to be part of the process to help youth develop into confident interdependent people who are able to function well in all aspects of society.

Brown has called for an Arctic university; there are colleges in many parts of the North. We have already trained 30 Inuit clergy at our Arthur Turner Training School in Pangnirtung, The College has moved to Iqaluit and is now operating in our Cathedral. It offers an accredited Diploma in Arctic Ministry through ATTS in association with Trinity School of Ministry at Ambridge, Pennsylvania.

Whether the First Nations of the Central Territory, the NWT, would provide water to the continent in a catastrophic crisis of climate change is a matter entirely under their control. The advent of domed cities in the Eastern Territory of Nunavut sometime in the next hundred years is as speculative as the addition of a Caribbean province to Canada, both discussed in the chapter which I am introducing.

But I can provide a dramatic example of northern Indigenous strength in the face of a development certain to take place, and equally as challenging. On August 29 of 2016 the largest ocean liner to traverse the Northwest Passage anchored off Cambridge Bay. Over a thousand tourists came ashore from the ten-storey cruise ship to a busy welcome. If Niagara Falls can handle 12 million tourists a year, any northern community can manage a few thousand.

Liberal colleagues and media in the south cringe because they imagine the poor, vulnerable and defenceless Inuit being swamped and losing everything, environmentally, culturally and economically. The local population had no such reservations and no difficulty. Chief Bellegarde is right in insisting that we get over thinking of Indigenous people as losers, unable to take care of business. In fact, the residents of the North have so much to share that their visitors may go home greatly enriched.

The Polaris deep water port serving Iqaluit is now under construction. Upon its completion, and with the building of two other deep water ports in the Arctic, there can be no doubt that the Northwest Passage will become a major tourist destination. In Iqaluit one imagines that the "Igloo Cathedral" will be a big draw, multiplying Sunday attendance in the summer, and boosting the turnout to our daily midweek services. Those visitors will be Christian guests and curious others, a situation similar to that at Westminster Abbey in England.

I have been asked if our members and clergy, mostly Inuit, could handle this influx without the cathedral losing its soul. To me this example is a parable of attitudes to the whole future of the North, the Indigenous peoples and of Canada itself. I can assure our readers that our northern people can handle anything and everything. I have described our people here as "proud, innovative and strong." We are ready for the future. Is the rest of Canada ready?

+ David W. Parsons

5

The Canadian Dream

A New Vision for our Capital City
Progressive Developments
First Nations First for a Change
Defending Arctic Sovereignty
The World is our Oyster
Domed Cities in the Arctic

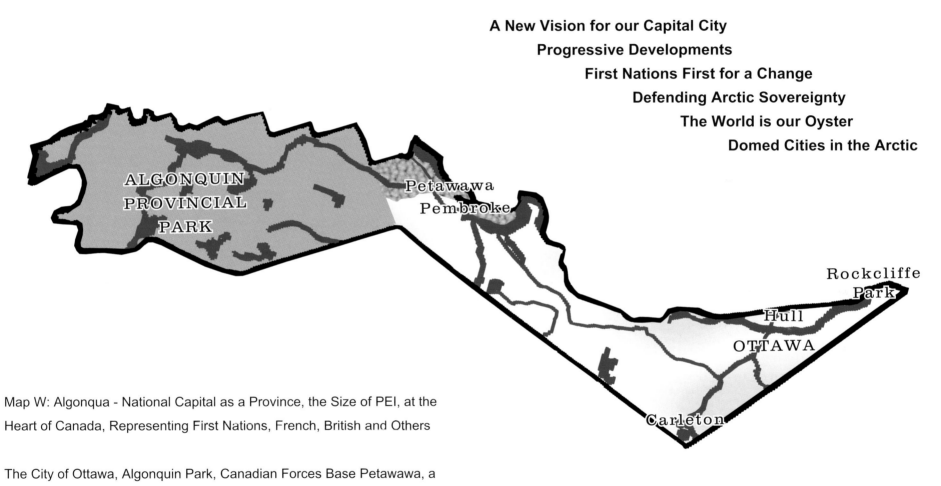

Map W: Algonqua - National Capital as a Province, the Size of PEI, at the Heart of Canada, Representing First Nations, French, British and Others

The City of Ottawa, Algonquin Park, Canadian Forces Base Petawawa, a Tiny Portion of Eastern Ontario and a Hull-Gatineau Smidgeon of Québec

To gain a bilingual province on its western flank, like New Brunswick to the east, a secure Québec of the twenty-first century might be ready at last to concede the city of Hull and a small slice of Gatineau to a new bilingual province called Algonqua. It might also include the city of Ottawa, a slice of Ontario, Canadian Forces Base Petawawa, and Algonquin Park. With a million people, Canada's capital should be sited in a bilingual province of natural parkland where New Canadians, French and English Canadians are happily secure. A province of Algonqua, including the traditional land base of the Algonquin people, would symbolize a new era with the full participation of First Nations in Confederation at last.

The policy of Diefenbaker Conservatives in opening Canada's doors to the world, which was later implemented by the Liberal Party, is an illustration of the First Nations style conconous politics described by John Ralston Saul as quoted by Elizabeth May. Despite raucous times in Question period, this is the way Canadians make social progress on important issues –a contrast to the American system in which immigration is not the only area of partisan paralysis and the resulting gridlock.

To give a more recent example, in 2016 the federal Liberals found inter-provincial and multi-party support for revisions to the Canada Pension Plan to increase future benefits for some 11 million workers, mostly younger, who have no workplace pension plans. They, the government, and their employers will all participate, thanks to agreement among nine of ten provinces and three territories (across the political spectrum!) plus support from three of five parties in the federal House of Commons.

This approach has worked for gender politics in government, and for gay marriage and gay ordination in two of the three largest Canadian church denominations. It is currently being applied to transgender issues – such a contrast with the USA where such issues are determined by politics based on fear rather than common sense. This approach is bearing fruit in physician assisted death and in legalization of marijuana as Canadians work to safeguard vulnerable young, disabled or older citizens.

Many Canadians aspire to national standards for child care, tuition free education, and "pharmacare." These advances will become possible only if and when Canadians are ready to enact them in the slow consensual system that works for us. Given the mood of the country "the next big thing" employing this approach may well be dramatic advancements among First Nations. The scope is as grand as any seaway, railroad or highway, but in this case the human dimension is especially to the fore.

Bishop David Parsons received his early education in Northern Labrador and has been employed even farther north since 1976, except for periods south and abroad for higher education and service assignments. He would insist that he learned more about life and what works in the real world in the North.

It is of interest that wise observers of the Canadian scene like Peter Mansbridge (from Churchill, Manitoba) and Pierre Berton (from Dawson City, Yukon) have said the same thing. It may be time for all Canadians to recognize our national sources of true wisdom.

Parsons has shown us the difference between quaint and profound in the analysis he offered of the painting, *Epiphany in the Snows* by Violet Teague. Equally significant is his contrast between the sunken *Erebus and Terror* ships of the Franklyn Expedition with 133 persons aboard, and the visit of the ten storey high *Crystal Serenity* bringing 1070 passengers plus a large crew into a new northern environment which most Canadians would hardly recognize. The former represent the harsh North most Canadians know, whereas the latter is a harbinger of things to come. The challenges are enormous but with faith, education, recognition of the resources involved and trust in the wisdom of Indigenous people, Canada is ready to move forward.

But progress is not yet uniform nor universal across the North. The situation there is not as dire as it is in Northern Ontario, or on the prairies, but neither is it as advanced as it is in the best examples from Québec and British Columbia. It is in Canada's best interests to make the investments (i.e. honour the treaties, settle land claims, pay our bills and facilitate self-government) appropriate to the situation.

The Indigenous Mi'kmaq people were prosperous and greatly impressed the first Europeans they met. They knew the Canadian Maritimes, from the Gaspé Peninsula to Cape Breton, by the name Mi'kma'ki, where they had lived productively and in peace, with a history back to the last Ice Age, some 13,000 years ago. Most Mi'kmaq families had two residences, one on the coast where they fished in the summer, and another inland for hunting moose and caribou in the winter. At peace with French Acadians, and frequently intermarrying, the Mi'kmaq were literate and happily Christian by the time the English arrived, determined to counter French and Catholic influence in the area.

In 1749 the first Canadian ancestors of the current writer were among 2,500 settlers, mostly poor and recruited mainly from England, arrived with dreams of a new beginning. They were settled on the opposite side of the harbor the Mi'kmaqs called Jipugtug, meaning "the biggest harbor," later Anglicized as Chebucto, until it was renamed for the Earl of Halifax who masterminded the expedition and designed the town. Its purpose in geo-politics was to counter French and Catholic influence in the region, and to prepare for the attack on Quebec in 1759.

The Mi'kmaq were used to a system of annual gifts from the French for use of their land. The English failed to adopt the system, leaving the Mi'kmag to resent the settlement of their land by immigrants without permission or pay. They refused to accept the authority of Governor Cornwallis who offered a bounty for anyone bringing in Mi'kmaq scalps, a practice imported from the British in New England … leaving the question of who were really the "savages."

After some rather eloquent correspondence, the Mi'kmaq declared war on the English and acquired weapons from the French in Louisbourg in Cape Breton. The English deported the Acadians and declared the Nova Scotia mainland off limits for the Mi'kmaq. Both actions succeeded at first, but within a generation the Acadians slipped back into unoccupied parts of the Maritime lands they loved and the Mi'maq signed a treaty which permitted occupation of certain remote portions of their old territory.

Nova Scotia is as close as it gets in Canada to one country, England, invading another, Mi'kma'ki, to take the property of residents by overwhelming force. Such actions are not tolerated in today's world, except perhaps in Crimea and parts of Georgia.

As a teenager in the Maritimes in the 1950s I often rode my bike 100 kilometres from Halifax to Truro through the Millbrook First Nations community on the edge of Truro, where my grandparents lived. Millbrook was and is an industrious and prosperous community where Indigenous teens have access to high school and college, and businesses flourish in an urban environment, using First Nations tax breaks to competitive advantage. Millbrook has been a predecessor to larger projects now, like the massive ten kilometre stretch of commercial developments currently under construction by the Tsuut'ina First Nation on Calgary's southwest Ring Road.

En route back to Halifax I would stop half way to visit relatives in a rural village where another reserve community existed, farther out on a dirt road, where education, health care and business opportunities were limited. Then as now, prostitution, drugs and gang activity provided what limited prospects there were, and my relatives were anxious to prevent me from venturing in that direction.

A Poverty Action Research Project of the Assembly of First Nations through Dalhousie University reported in 2016 on attempts by First Nations individuals to remedy the situation. "In the past, the economic development approach of the Shubenacadie First Nation has been through stand-alone business and employment initiatives. Over the years, the band has implemented a number of business schemes, including a saw mill, a poultry farm, a pig farm and a bean sprout farm, a grocery store, a fishery supply store, a building supply store, and cabinetry training and supply, to name a few. These endeavours have tended to be implemented with the best of intentions, but over the long-run have not been successful. Reasons for this include the fact that each was an isolated project not directly tied to any set of community initiatives or goals, a lack of consumer support from the community and surrounding area, and the realities of a being a rural community."

The answer is clearly not found in individual efforts in areas of business already in jeopardy among neighbours engaged is similar enterprises. The successful solutions will be political and systemic, but political clout and full benefits of treaty resources remain elusive. The report continues. "The community is politically divided, a situation which has proven detrimental to achieving health and prosperity. Most people agree that eradicating poverty and promoting economic development is an important goal to work towards, but the community cannot agree on how to go about achieving this goal. Some believe privately owned businesses are the way to move forward, while others believe that band owned businesses for revenue and job creation are more likely to benefit the community as a whole."

Until the resources become available a sense of futility prevails. "Further complicating community relationships and decision making is the lack of a community supported vision and/or strategy for community development, economic development or even community well-being. Without a vision and strategy in place, the people do not have a coherent set of goals to work towards that guide the decision-making process for any initiative or activity proposed or considered by the government."

Gangs are now called "associations" in many places. Society is now legalizing certain drugs, and "sex workers" are regarded by many as being engaged in a high risk occupation, deserving protection. But life in communities like this First Nation remains tough. Adequate services and business investment could conceivably change all that if systemic implementations of treaty rights and self-government could replace the current "welfare state" of affairs.

Millbrook has found systemic approaches like certain other First Nations advancements dotted across the country in piecemeal fashion, but this is not adequate or even just in reference to others left behind. Typically, some of my racist relatives regard the Millbrook situation with anger because of the tax breaks, whereas the government of Nova Scotia uses tax breaks to lure other industries to the province. It provides subsidies to some, in the belief that such systems have wider benefits to the whole community. The time has come for a systemic approach to First Nations that is legal, just, workable and beneficial across Canada.

While studying for the ministry at McGill University I had a brief internship one summer at the United Church in the First Nations community of Kahnawake, across the river from Montréal. My first-ever funeral took place on my first day, when I learned how easy it is to lead the singing of familiar hymns in Mohawk phonetics. After the service Chief Horne, chair of the local church board, offered me the choice of vehicles for my work.

I could have either his new Cadillac or his old Ford Thunderbird. I chose to use the bus.

This Indigenous leader helped me to understand the prosperity of this community whose territory straddles the border with the United States, enjoying the benefits of free trade before anyone else, thanks to the old Jay Treaty negotiated by Joseph Brant. This particular First Nation used to be criticized for "gaming the system" in this way, but a similar deal was signed for all Canadians just twenty-five years later.

Meanwhile, ten First Nations plus the Inuit communities numbering 150,000 people in Québec account for approximately 2% of that population of the province. Almost none have any such advantages except for the Cree communities in the north which are fully employed and as prosperous as Kahnawake through contracts negotiated with Québec Hydro which is thrilled with the agreements.

We are proposing treaty settlements and self-governments with resource control which would extend such opportunities and prosperity to all those who signed the still-unimplemented treaties across the country, instead of these few piecemeal arrangements benefiting a few First Nations who have found ways to work the system, leaving others clinging to existence.

Late in my career I ministered in Owen Sound, Ontario during intense court cases and ultimately successful efforts by First Nations to exclusive fishing rights in nearby portions of the Great Lakes, as "guaranteed" in long neglected treaties. I attended protests and rallies with First Nations folk despite criticism by those who objected to their "claiming rights that other Canadians don't have." As a Maritimer I was well acquainted with provisions which limited fishing licenses to Aboriginals and to non-Aboriginals with historic permits in certain areas. This causes some distress there too, but it is a supply management system that had been negotiated in good faith. In Ontario that kind of negotiation had concluded a century ago but was not enforced, leaving First Nations to live by their wits or by what seemed like handouts.

I was proud of Warren Lougheed, the main fish processor (who shipped his products to Boston) when he courageously risked the anger of friends and neighbours to buy fish only from First Nations while court cases and protests raged. In fact, he was recognizing the benefits of dealing with First Nations systemically, according to just application of the law. This is the approach we are proposing, not piecemeal but everywhere in Canada, confident in First Nations abilities and the availability of appropriate resources.

It has taken longer to reach this point on the prairies, and the stakes are higher there. Without this kind of accommodation and reconciliation with a large and growing First Nations presence, the present prosperity of the West is almost certain to produce a "Mississippi syndrome" of a police state, incarceration, drugs, gangs, prostitution and slums.

Many Westerners see only the derelict results of our history, as many members of First Nations continue in lifestyles they would gladly exchange for the Indigenous fishers of Owen Sound, the Indigenous hydro workers of Québec, or the prosperous First Nations businesses in the few Maritime locations where some kind of systemic approach has worked.

My church denomination has been led by a First Nations national "moderator" in Stan McKay from the McKay clan in Manitoba, mentioned earlier. The Very Rev. Stan Mckay led the United Church of Canada as well as any Moderator in history, so self-government is not now at issue, any more than it was in the time of Louis Riel and James McKay. The current governmental systems do not work for First Nations in any coherent fashion, but we can see the way forward.

Finally, permit me to illustrate how the system works for some and fails for others in British Columbia and the north of the Pacific region. I had the privilege of serving as founding chair of the Board of Governors of a four campus community college in the 1970s, centred in Dawson Creek with sites throughout the north. One board member from the middle of the Alaska Highway was a prominent, successful and highly respected lawyer with an obvious concern for community life.

Over several years his firm had represented a First Nations band in an ultimately successful land claim with respect to oil and gas reserves being explored by an American oil company. After years of work, he won a settlement of one hundred million dollars and nobody was anything other than delighted and impressed with his 20% fee. The town was happy. The college had a new benefactor. The First Nation was happy. The American investors smiled at their prospects all the way to the bank. The system worked!

In the present era, First Nations are represented in court and in other negotiations by more than one thousand Indian, Inuit and Métis lawyers who are members of the Indigenous Bar Association of Canada, which includes federal Justice Minister Jody Wilson-Raybould. Other Canadians have not all adjusted to this reality, and there is a howl if the government or any corporation pays a First Nations legal firm fees even half the twenty million earned by the firm of my friend in Fort Nelson, BC.

I am among the many who find the outrageous salaries paid to some sports figures, some movie stars, some doctors, some politicians and some lawyers to be obscene. But we have a double standard when it comes to First Nations where lawyers, politicians and business leaders now sometimes make a lot of money, as do certain other Canadians. We need to get used to First Nations millionaires, perhaps not many but certainly some, as we establish systems that provide level playing fields for all Canadians throughout society, rich, poor and most of us somewhere in between.

The first French settlement in Canada was established at Port Royal in Nova Scotia in 1605 by Samuel de Champlain. The first English settlement in Canada was established at Cupids, Newfoundland in 1610 by John Guy. In the 150 years since Confederation, people from all over the world have settled here in the country Bishop David Parsons calls "our home on native land," a semi-humorous additional "revision" to a phrase in our anthem.

We are proud of what has happened here for the most part, but for the next 150 years we are looking to make history in relation to Indigenous people who have been in Canada since time immemorial.

The first mega infrastructure project in Canada was the building of a railway linking the confederal provinces to British Columbia at a cost of about 2 billion dollars, all told, 140 years ago, or almost 100 billion in today's dollars, a worthy endeavour but one which came perilously close to bankrupting the country.

The second was the Alaska Highway, at something under 2 billion 70 years ago, until we add the paving and maintenance costs, but otherwise we got it free ... worth some 75 billion today. The St. Lawrence Seaway was a bargain at 3 billion, or some 75 billion in today's dollars. The benefits to British Collumbia, Alaska and Ontario are uncalculatable.

Treaties and land claims with Indigenous people, before confederation and since, were worth some 1.25 billion then, or nearly 100 billion in today's dollars. The human cost of this unpaid debt has been born by Indigenous Canadians all these years. They win every case that finally wends its way through the courts, but the interest is mounting, at a cost to the nation as a whole. There can be no doubt that Indigenous leaders are ready, willing and able to manage these funds in self-government for education, health, living standards and sustainable development of resources needed by Canada and the world. A oap of 100 billion dollars to settle all legitimate claims and provide the initial infrastructure required for proper development of Canada's resources is as affordable as the railway, the highway and the seaway. It is doable within a manageable addition to the national debt in a Canada-wide and Canada-high venture which will benefit the whole country. This will happen in the short term or the long term, and the First Nations are patient. Can the rest of the country wait?

Meanwhile, even further north, in August of 2007 a metallic Russian flag was placed on the Arctic Ocean seabed at the North Pole by the crew of the Mir-1 mini submarine.

The crew and scientists were accompanied by military officials and members of the Russian Parliament. They were attempting to forestall territorial claims by Canada, and even Denmark, United States and Norway (all members of NATO), as to who has the rights to mineral and carbon resources under the ocean floor at this site.

This is a potentially lucrative oil and gas area and Russia's ambitions for territorial expansion of late may not be limited to Georgia, Crimea and Ukraine. Our illustration of the Russian flag is based on media reports at the time and is produced by a Canadian high school student who managed to catch the illusion of an underwater environment near the Lomonosov Ridge at a site which is certainly much closer to the Canadian shoreline than to any part of Russia.

Without over-reacting, alarming the public or appearing to take the flag incident too seriously, Canada filed an application with the United Nations to expand its own Atlantic sea boundary under the Law of the Sea Convention. Canada also responded to the Russians by dispatching two scientifically equipped icebreakers, the *Terry Fox* and the *Louis S. St-Laurent*, on a six-week mission to map a portion of the Arctic seabed at Lomonosov Ridge, the heart of the contested area.

Watercolour by Ariel Sinton, Uxbridge, Ontario

In a news release, then Foreign Affairs Minister John Baird said "As demonstrated by these planned surveys, our government is committing the resources necessary to ensure that Canada secures international recognition of the full extent of its continental shelf." The report quotes then Environment Minister Leona Aglukkaq, a prominent Inuit leader, saying, "Our government is expanding our economic and scientific opportunities by defining Canada's last frontier. This is important to Canadians, especially those in the North, as their future and their prosperity is at stake." The current government of Canada remains in accord with these positions.

Glacial ice continues to melt rapidly due to climate change and anthropogenic warming, opening up vast energy resources via now-accessible waterways traditionally regarded as Canadian.

In 2009 the U.S. Geological Survey estimated the Arctic contains 30 percent of global gas reserves and 13 percent of undiscovered oil, and we know very well that oil has been a factor in otherwise unnecessary wars elsewhere in recent years.

The United Nations Convention on the Law of the Sea has ruled that coastal nations have exclusive economic rights to natural resources located within 200 nautical miles of their shores. A petition may be presented to extend any nation's zone to 350 nautical miles if the country can provide proof that its continental shelf stretches from sovereign territory to beyond the allotted distance. International conferences are ongoing in these regards.

Russian President Vladimir Putin has an aggressive position regarding the Lomonosov Ridge, insisting that this undersea formation, named after a famous Russian academic, and extending from our Ellesmere Island to their New Siberian Islands, belongs to Russia. He had the flag planted despite the fact that the geographic North Pole is closer to Canada and the Magnetic North Pole is within Canada without question at present.

Speaking in a National Security Council meeting in April, 2014 President Putin described the Arctic as "a sphere of our special interest." In almost threatening language Putin stated, "Given the circumstances, we need to take additional measures so as not to fall behind our partners, to maintain Russia's influence in the region and maybe, in some areas, to get ahead of our partners. These are our priority tasks." These words are similar to his words prior to action in Crimea and Ukraine.

Canadians repelled three invasions from a neighbour in earlier times, has served in two world wars and has led peacekeeping missions in the twentieth century. We "stand on guard" for Canada but we may find our peacekeeping skills put to the test in the Arctic.

Robert Huebert, a professor at the University of Calgary's Centre for Strategic Studies, said in a 2014 interview in the *Globe and Mail* that "overlapping claims in the Arctic will likely lead to tough negotiations." The situation is delineated in the Arctic maps on Map X of this book, to which our readers might refer again at this point.

Huebert said, "Deteriorating relations between Russia and the West over the ongoing crisis in eastern Ukraine could prompt Russian leaders to see Canadian activities in the north as NATO provocations. I would suspect they would see this as a continuation of western encirclement. It may be at this point where Putin is willing to push back."

Before long we may have to demonstrate willingness to "stand on guard" for ourselves in the North by deployment of our military, a show of strength like that of Canadian troops now facing Russia in the Baltic states. Should we be invaded, our membership in NATO should certainly come into play once our claims, based on science and international law, are verified by the UN.

This in itself may contribute to our ability to "talk our way out of this" once again.

Canada, Denmark, Norway, Russia and USA now have sovereignty over Arctic Ocean areas within 200 nautical miles of their coastlines. A vast area is ready for sustainable development once Artic sovereignty is established.

The Sector Proposal by the USA, which makes the North Pole the central dividing point, mainly at Canada's expense, without much scientific support beyond the influence of The United States over smaller voting nations at the UN.

The Meridian Line Proposal: Arctic borders extended to midpoint, favored by Denmark, Canada and perhaps acceptable to Norway and Russia under Law of the Sea Conventions to be adjudicated by the UN in the present decade.

Map X

So if Canada is confident of extending its territory by expanding into the Arctic Ocean in the North, why not expand to the South by including the Turks and Caicos Islands in the Caribbean? Once a hideaway for the rich and famous of this country, these islands are now accessible and popular with the travelling public, wealthy or on a budget. The islanders are as fond of Canadians as we are of them.

Romantic references state that the Turks and Caicos Islands were named for the Turks after Ottoman-era Turkish pirates, and Caicos relating to the Spanish term for cays or keys, but no one is sure where the name came from. What we do know is that wealthier Canadian families have vacationed and invested there since the nineteenth century and other Canadians are now ready to be included.

In 1917, on the fiftieth anniversary of confederation, while Canadian Prime Minister Robert Borden was vacationing on the islands, he suggested that the Turks and Caicos join Canada. He repeated this as a "demand" at the 1919 Paris Peace Conference. His entreaty was rejected by British Prime Minister David Lloyd George.

The islands were a dependency of Jamaica until its independence in 1962 when they asked to be freed. The British do not know what to do with these islands, but Canadians do. They were assigned to the Bahamas until they also gained independence in 1973. At that point they reverted to control of the British Foreign Office in London, with local self-government on minor issues.

Max Saltzman, a New Democratic Party Member of Parliament, introduced a private member's bill in 1974 to annex the islands to Canada, but it did not pass in the Canadian House of Commons. In 2004 Conservative MP Peter Goldring led a fact finding mission to the Turks and Caicos to explore the possibility once more. He drafted a motion asking the Canadian Government to look into the issue, but his party declined to adopt it as a priority.

In May of 2014 Turks and Caicos Premier Rufus Ewing was hosted by Canadian parliamentarians at public meetings in Toronto's Westin Harbour Castle. The premier also visited the Canadian Parliament, looking to improve the Turks and Caicos relationship with Canada. After meetings with Prime Minister Stephen Harper, he pronounced himself open to a possible "marriage" in the future … and the discussion continues.

The eight main islands, 30 smaller islands and hundreds of coral reefs have a total land area of 616.3 square kilometres, even smaller than Prince Edward Island. But they have 332 square kilometres of beach front, mostly developed now as affordable public resorts, with expensive private vacation property further out on smaller islands.

In its ocean setting, the total global "footprint" of the Turks and Caicos is larger than PEI. The weather is always ideal with 350 days of sun each year. Agricultural products include maize, beans, tapioca and citrus fruits. Fish, shellfish and conch are the only significant export, with some $2,000,000. of lobster, oyster, dried and fresh conch, and conch shells exported annually, primarily to Canada, but also to the United Kingdom and the United States.

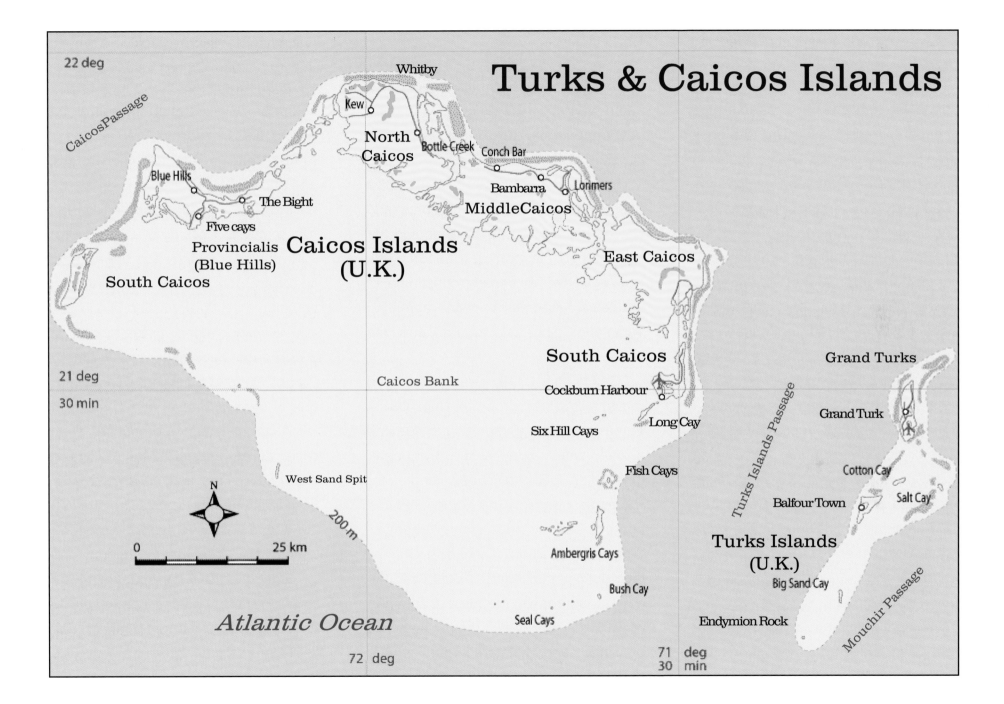

Map Y: Turks and Caicos Islands: The Best Kept Secret of Wealthy Canadians Could Become Canada's Oyster, Open and Available to All

Aside from tourism, the main industry is financial services in this emerging "Singapore of the West." The territory's currency is the United States dollar in this offshore "tax haven," which has scrupulously avoided the taint of money-laundering by American, Canadian and British international traders and investors. With 10,000 companies headquartered here, the Turks and Caicos have no need to impose any income tax on their citizens. Is Canada ready for a tax free province?

As a British territory, its sovereign is Queen Elizabeth II, represented by a governor appointed by the monarch on the advice of the British Foreign Office. The United Nations Special Committee on De-colonization includes this territory on the UN list of Non-Self-Governing Territories, and there is local support for a union with Canada.

The idea of union was brought up yet again in Canada in 1986 by Conservative MP Dan McKenzie, but it was rejected by his party's caucus committee on external affairs in 1987. However, the Canadian government has never dismissed the possibility of a future union.

In 2004 the province of Nova Scotia passed legislation to invite Turks and Caicos to join that province, should the islands become part of Canada. This was designed to bypass constitutional problems associated with admitting Turks and Caicos as a separate province at the outset.

On March 2, 2009, the Ottawa Citizen ran an online article reporting the interest of the Canadian government in opening a deep-water port in the Caribbean that would facilitate "a new market for Canadian goods in the Caribbean and nearby Central and South America." Without naming the Turks and Caicos, the article continued, "Suppose the port, unaffordable for most Caribbean countries, boosted their standard of living and bolstered hemispheric security. Suppose the port doubled as a Canadian military operations base for countries wanting help to patrol their waters and to interdict the Caribbean's robust trade in smuggled arms, drugs and people."

From 1950 to 1981, the United States had a missile tracking station on Grand Turk. It was transferred to the American space program, NASA, after John Glenn completed his three earth orbits in 1962, successfully landed in the ocean and was brought back ashore to Grand Turk Island. Canada's aerospace industry is one of the most advanced in the world, with annual sales approaching twenty billion dollars. Based in Montreal, its only drawback is the lack of an aerospace oceanfront launch centre. The one in the Turks and Caicos is available, no longer used by NASA but ideally situated for us.

Since the 2010 earthquake in Haiti a small French speaking community has developed a presence, making union with Canada even more attractive from an island governance perspective.

David Anderson, Parliamentary Secretary to Canada's Minister of Foreign Affairs, and Ricardo Don Hue Gardiner, Minister of Border Control and Labour of the Turks and Caicos Islands, co-chaired the first meeting of the Canada-Turks and Caicos Islands Bilateral Working Group, held in Ottawa on May 28, 2015.

Just eight of the islands are inhabited, with the remainder preserved under ecological protection of coral reefs, though open to limited sport fishing and boating as a water park. In 2010, a total of 245 cruise ships arrived at the Grand Turk Cruise Terminal, carrying a total of nearly a million visitors.

The Providenciales International Airport is the main entry point for the Turks and Caicos Islands. There are seven airports, with one located on each of the main inhabited islands except one, connected by a causeway. A full range of technological amenities serves the Turks and Caicos business and residential communities with mobile phone services, internet, radio,

Canada-Turks and Caicos Parliamentary Working Group

television and newspaper media.

The French vacation company *Club Mediterannee* (Club Med) has an all-inclusive adult resort called "Turkoise" on the main island. Several Hollywood stars have built homes in the Turks and Caicos, including Dick Clark, Bruce Willis, Ben Affleck and Eva Longoria.

Canadians looking for the perfect vacation spot will be interested to know that last year the island, which includes the capital city of the Turks and Caicos, was named the second best island in the world by Travelers' Choice Awards. Perhaps it is time for more of us to check out the possibilities.

Grace Bay on Provencialis Island, Turks and Caicos … Described as "the Best Beach in the World" with Probably Many Canadians in this Picture

Those who study the issue always seem to see clear benefits to the islands themselves in joining Canada. The benefits to Canada are in having our own financial "Singapore" where money and taxes stay in our country, and in having our own tropical "Hawaii" where people can vacation securely and have access to Canadian Health Care, which is practically identical to the first class services now available in Turks and Caicos. A new hospital, opened in the capital city of "Provo" in 2010, is administered from Toronto by Interhealth Canada, with triannual certification by Accreditation Canada, most recently in 2012 and 2015.

The population of the Turks and Caicos is 50,000, the same as Labrador, a figure we have begun to think of as the threshold for eventual provincial status. Public Education is mandatory in Turks and Caicos for children aged five to sixteen. The Turks and Caicos Islands Community College offers tuition-free higher education to students who have completed their secondary education. Once any student completes studies at Turks and Caicos Islands Community College, they are offered government bursaries to further their education at any university in USA, Canada, or the United Kingdom, at no cost to the students.

The main religious affiliation in these islands is Baptist at 33% of the population, with approximately 10% Catholic, 10% Methodist, 10% Anglican, 11% Pentecostal, 8% other Christian, 7% no religion, and smaller numbers associated with the one synagogue, one mosque and one Hindu temple in the capital city.

There are no immediate plans to further the prospect for union between Turks and Caicos and Canada, but it is sensible enough and attractive enough for us to imagine it happening before Canada's 2067 bicentennial, 50 years from now at the latest. Why should we wait so long?

After a look at the changes a hundred years could bring to the map of Canada, we will conclude this 2017 sesquicentennial exhibition with a *grand finale* of sorts.

That vision of domed communities in the North is not more ambitious than a ribbon of steel rail from coast to coast in the nineteenth century, and no more impossible than building a highway 1700 miles from south to northwest in 170 days. We are the people who built the St. Lawrence Seaway some 300 nautical miles from the centre of the country to the open sea in the twentieth century. Come on, Canada; let's dream big!

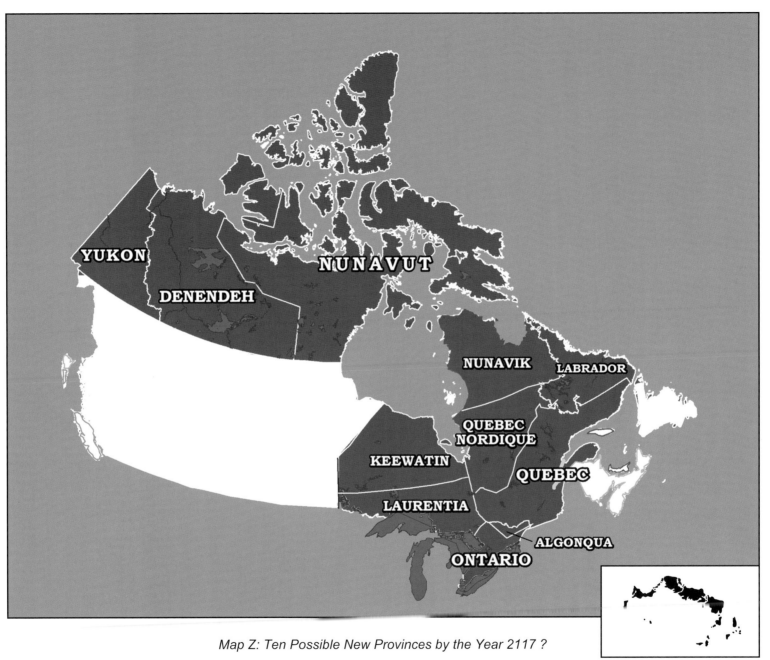

Map Z: Ten Possible New Provinces by the Year 2117 ?

Turks & Caicos Islands

The poet, Samuel Taylor Coleridge, could not possibly have imagined Yukon, the Northwest Territories and Nunavut as the most likely settings for domed cities with comfortable lifestyles in controlled environments. Yet the river at the ends of the earth may turn out to be the fabled Northwest Passage as it comes to life. The mines of the north are certainly "cavernous" and the Arctic itself is indeed a "sunless sea" for much of the year.

The mineral strikes around Voisey's Bay have the potential to turn Labrador from a region with among the lowest per capita incomes in Canada into the highest in the country, as happened in Yukon and the island of Newfoundland in succession some years ago. In Nunavut the tiny population of 33,000 is the fastest growing in Canada through natural increase and immigration, and the Indigenous majority has negotiated complete control of natural resources in an area the size of Quebec. This means that one strike the size of Voisey's Bay or the Ring of Fire could provide an instant payoff of more than one million dollars per household, making Nunavut potentially a Kuwait North.

Life in domed cities has been considered for years as the only practical way of colonizing Mars or Venus, a prospect now considered likely within decades. In Antarctica, geodesic domes are tall enough for radar towers, and they have been able to withstand winds of 200 mph for over 25 years. Americans think Alaska can function well without domes and Russia appears unwilling to make the investment. Domes in the Canadian North are likely to appear first at mining sites large enough to require a village sized labor force, with one exception to be considered as a proto-type.

For that matter, all but one of 28 settlements, which include virtually 100% of the population of Nunavut, could fit inside domed structures smaller than the Skydome sports complex in Toronto. With a retractable dome for airing out in the summer, or for psychological reasons important to human beings, life in the long winters could be most pleasurable in the North later in this century.

Living and working environments could be the very best in the world, rather than among the worst. Conditioned air would replace cooped up winter atmospheres.

There could be full spectrum lighting sixteen hours a day instead of months of darkness. People could enjoy year-round gardens and country club amenities like tennis courts and swimming pools, or whatever the Inuit, their employees and their neighbours choose. Pollution from diamond, gold, nickel, copper and silver mines could be dealt with cleanly in such controlled environments.

Science fiction has long presented either space or the bottom of the sea as the last frontier. Who knows where successful northern experiences could lead by the end of this century in Canada? Jules Verne's depictions of airplane travel in *Around the World in Eighty Days*, submarines in *Twenty Thousand Leagues Under the Sea*, and a space voyage called *From the Earth to the Moon* were all greeted with incredulous glee a hundred years ago. All these materialized in the twentieth century with uncanny accuracy. Please quote this book when you see domed cities.

The resources of the North and the creative application of existing technology could make the vision of domed communities a reality within the lifetimes of young Inuit, Indian and Métis peoples and their employees from the south in what we might describe as giant igloos.

If there is one candidate to be the first settlement under a dome anywhere in the world, it would be on Ellesmere Island, a large island with two tiny hamlets, a village, a Canadian Forces base and a total population of less than 200 persons.

Only tiny Kaffeklubben Island (Coffee Club Island) north of Greenland is further north on this planet, but it has no permanent residents, no prospects for development and there are good reasons for it to be preserved as is.

Ellesmere Island is not as large as Labrador but larger than the island of Newfoundland. No knowledgeable analysts doubt that Ellesmere Island is a storehouse of resources needed throughout the world, now capable of development in contained, economically viable and environmentally sound ways.

Canadian Forces Station Alert, also known as CFS Alert, is a Canadian Armed Forces signals intelligence intercept facility located in Alert, Nunavut, on the northeastern tip of Ellesmere Island. With a population of 75, it is the northernmost permanently inhabited place on earth. Alert is ripe for a dome, both for the comfort and security of its inhabitants and for experimentation in living in an environment remarkably similar to Mars. Canada's next contribution to space exploration may appropriately begin here.

As the Most Northerly Settlement on Earth, Alert, Nunavut is Ready for its Dome

> The shadow of the dome of pleasure
> Floated midway on the waves;
> Where was heard the mingled measure
> From the fountain and the caves.
> It was a miracle of rare device,
> A sunny pleasure dome with caves of ice.

Acknowledgments

Editing by David Bruce and Jenny Sutacriti Brown

Proofreading by Anne Bauman, Helen Macdonald and Patty Berube.

Advance Review Copies by Sheri Rotchill

Cover and Page design by Salvador Ayala

Biblical phrase "weeping and wailing and gnashing of dentures" as amended by Jenny Sutacriti Brown

Technical assistance by Len Guelke in producing the maps based on the Lambert Azimuthal Equal-Area Projection

Technical assistance by David Monihan for Map X, originally produced for *Canadian Geographic Magazine,* used by permission

Illustrations

Front Cover Map: by Jen Adomeit; purchase online at www.JenAdomeit.com or from esty.com

The map on page 1 is © ODT, Inc. in 2002…excerpted from the South-up version, first published and copyrighted in 2010.
More information available at: www.ManyWaysToSeeTheWorld.org
For maps and other related teaching materials contact: ODT, Inc., PO Box 134, Amherst MA 01004 USA;
(800-736-1293; Fax: 413-549-3503; E-mail: odtstore@odt.org)

Maps not listed below illustrating the shape of Canada and development of provinces and territories in the 19th, 20th and 21st are based on the Lambert Azimuthal Equal-Area Projection, executed with the assistance of Len Guelke.

Map D © ODT, Inc. 2015. ODTmaps video which explains the Population Map is at: https://www.youtube.com/watch?v=rhqGlV4I8qU
More information available at: www.ManyWaysToSeeTheWorld.org
For maps and other related teaching materials contact: ODT, Inc., PO Box 134, Amherst MA 01004 USA;
(800-736-1293; Fax: 413-549-3503; E-mail: odtstore@odt.org)

Map series E is reproduced by permission of the Canadian Hydrographic Services

Map F of Iraq is used with the permission of Judicial Watch

Map G Published in Germany in 1934 is in the public domain.

Map M of the Haldimand Tract Proclamation courtesy of Six Nations Lands and Resources

Map O of First Nations in Canada is an amalgam of ideas borrowed from Indian and Northern Affairs Canada and other sources.

Map X reproduced from the Canadian Geographic Magazine by permission

Map Y by "retiredexpats" courtesy Turks and Caicos Tourist Board

Photo of Inuvik Mosque by the Toronto Star

Photos of Notre Dame Basilica are deemed to be in the public domain

Photos of United Churches are deemed to be in the public domain

Photos of St. Jude's Anglican Cathedral are presented courtesy of Douglas Doak, Executive Officer, Diocese of the Arctic

Image of the Painting of Epiphany in the Snows by Violet Teague is in the public domain

Photo of Canada-Turks and Caicos Parliamentary Working Group from Foreign Affairs, Trade and Development, Canada

Photo of Providenciales, courtesy Turks and Caicos Board of Tourism

The Russian Flag was drawn by Ariel Sinton

The Photo of Alert by F.B. Edison is used with his permission

About the Contributors

Perry Bellegarde is the recipient of the Queen's Jubilee Medal (2012), Saskatchewan Medal (2005), Queen's Jubilee Medal (2002) and Confederation Medal (1992). In 1984, Bellegarde graduated from the University of Regina with a Bachelor of Administration. In March 2012, he graduated from the Certified Corporate Board Training through The Directors College sponsored by the Conference Board of Canada and McMaster University's DeGroote School of Business. Bellegarde's leadership as National Chief of the Assembly of First Nations is based on a vision that includes processes for self-determination and recognition of inherent Aboriginal and Treaty rights within Canada.

Ward Kaiser, internationally known for his expertise in map interpretation, introduced the Peters Projection – "the map that revolutionized the practice of cartography" - to North America in 1983. As an area-accurate map, it promotes "fairness for all peoples" and has since become one of the most widely recognized projections ever devised. Kaiser's background includes experience as a publisher, business executive, church leader, syndicated columnist, lecturer and social activist. His latest book, *How Maps Change Things: A Conversation about the Maps We Choose and the World We Want*, is published by CopperHouse/Wood Lake Publications in Kelowna, BC, by ODT Inc. in the USA, by New Internationalist in Australia and the UK and in a Thai translation in Bangkok. He previously co-authored a book marking Canada's 100th Birthday.

Elizabeth May is the leader of the Green Party of Canada. An environmentalist, author, activist, and lawyer, she served as the Executive Director of the Sierra Club of Canada from 1989 to 2006, when she was elected to the leadership of the forward looking Green Party. As the member of Parliament representing Saanich-Gulf Islands she lives in Sidney, British Columbia, though her family home is at the other end of the country, in Margaree Harbour, Cape Breton Island, giving Elizabeth May a truly national pan-Canadian perspective.

The Hon. Rob Nicholson is regarded by many as the dean of the Conservative party of Canada. First elected as Member of Parliament from Niagara Falls in 1984, he served the Mulroney government as Parliamentary Secretary and held cabinet posts in the Campbell and Harper governments as Minister of Science, Minister of Small Business, Government House leader, Minister of Justice, Attorney General for Canada, Minister of Defense, and Minister of Foreign Affairs. Nicholson is uniquely qualified to describe Canada's image and our place in the world.

The Hon. Larry Bagnell is the popular longstanding member of parliament representing the constituency of Yukon with responsibilities for northern development, infrastructure and First Nations participation. As the Vice Chair of the Standing Committee of Parliamentarians of Arctic Regions, Bagnell is Canada's authority on international northern affairs and Canada's place in the world in this regard.

The Rt. Rev. David Parsons is the Bishop of the Arctic for the Anglican Church of Canada. Distinguished now by his flowing white beard, Parsons rose through the ranks of Threshold Ministries and was consecrated at the "Igloo Cathedral" of St. Jude in Iqaluit in 2012 after a lengthy ministry with his wife Rita and their sons in the Church of the Ascension in Inuvik, NWT.

During the national unity crisis of the 1970s and 80s, Brian Arthur Brown provided insightful observation in *Separatism*, with a substantial foreword by Québec Premier René Lévesque, its answer in *The New Confederation*, with BC Premier W.A.C. Bennett, concluding with *The Canadian Challenge*, based on 1,000 radio editorials broadcast daily from Vancouver to Hamilton on 16 stations of the Moffat Communications Network. Always writing collaboratively, in *True North, Strong and Free*, Brown goes full circle in analysis of Canada's interesting history, dynamic present and promising future, assuming that Quebec is probably here to stay now, and reaching out to First Nations for a similar resolution of long-standing grievances and lost opportunities.

Brown is the author of over 20 books on the quest for peace and harmony between First Nations and other Canadians, French and English in Canada, Canadians and Americans at war and in peace, and Jews, Christians and

Brian Arthur Brown

Muslims worldwide. His *magnum opus* is a bestselling two-volume compendium *Three Testaments: Torah, Gospel and Quran* (2012) and *Four Testaments: Tao Te Ching, Analects, Dhammapada, Bhagavad Gita* (2016), both from the Rowman and Littlefield Publishing Group. This set is of particular interest and some

importance since "faith relations" have joined "race relations" as the hot button issues of the twenty first century.

Brown holds a bachelor's degree in Classics from Dalhousie University in Halifax, a master's degree in Theology from McGill University in Montréal, a doctorate in Organizational Behavior from the University of California, and has done post-doctoral Studies in Executive Leadership at Harvard University. He is currently a member of the Oxford Round Table at Oxford University and in 2015 he was elected as a fellow of the Royal Society for the Arts. Like Ward Kaiser, the curator of maps for this book, Brown is a minister of the United Church of Canada. Married for over fifty years, Brian and Jenny Brown live within earshot of the thunderous Niagara Falls where Brian currently serves as Scholar-in-Residence for the historic and progressive First Baptist Church in Niagara Falls, NY and Minister Emeritus at St. John's-Stevensville United Church in Fort Erie, Ontario.

In Sesquicentennial Solidarity with Inuit, Métis, First Nations and Others in the North

Inuit and other members of St. Jude's "Igloo Cathedral" in Iqaluit, and supporting congregations all over the Arctic, together with friends in the south and abroad, hope to finish paying the ten-million-dollar cost of re-building the Cathedral of the Arctic in 2017. This is a challenging endeavor with over two hundred and fifty thousand dollars remaining, and repayment slowed by rising costs of various ministries. Other Canadians who wish to share in that goal in solidarity with this vision of northern vitality as part of their personal or family sesquicentennial celebration are encouraged to join generously in this undertaking. Proceeds from the sale of this book are also dedicated to this purpose. Cheques may be made to The Diocese of the Arctic (with "Cathedral Building Fund" in the memo) and mailed to the business office at The Diocese of the Arctic, Box 190, Yellowknife, NWT X1A 2N2. Tax deductible receipts will be mailed to addresses as provided.